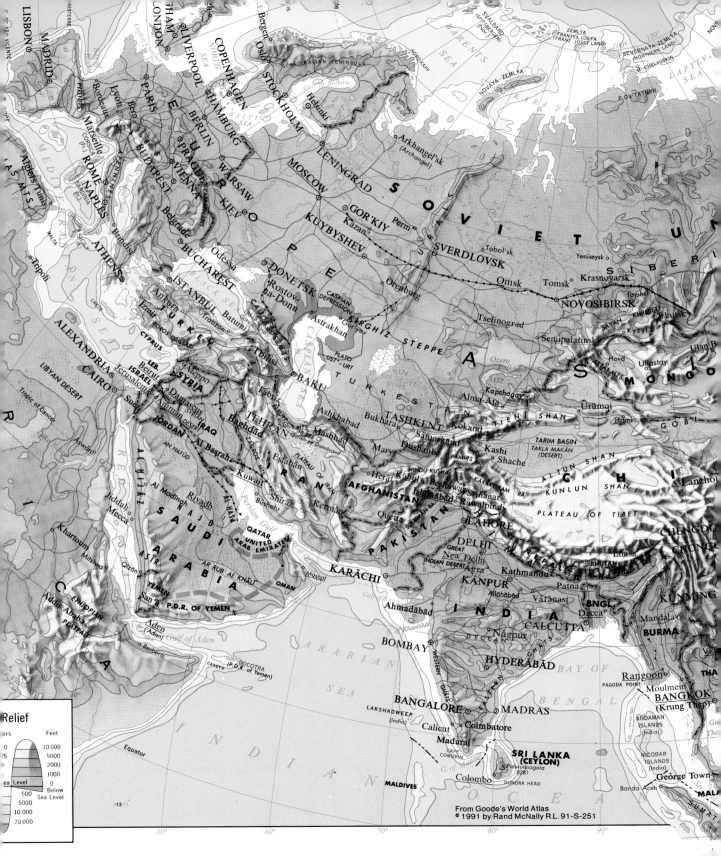

Relief

From Goode's World Atlas
© 1991 by Rand McNally R.L. 91-S-251

Enchantment of the World

SRI LANKA

By Robert Zimmermann

Consultant for Sri Lanka: Joan D. Winship, M.A., Augustana College, Department of Political Science, Rock Island, Illinois

Consultant for Reading: Robert L. Hillerich, Ph.D., Visiting Professor, University of South Florida; Consultant, Pinellas County Schools, Florida

CHILDRENS PRESS®
CHICAGO

Tea leaves are spread out to dry.

Project Editor: Mary Reidy
Design: Margrit Fiddle

Library of Congress Cataloging-in-Publication Data

Zimmermann, Robert (Robert B.)
  Sri Lanka / by Robert Zimmermann.
    p.   cm. — (Enchantment of the world)
  Includes index.
  Summary: Describes the geography, history, culture,
industry, and people of Sri Lanka.
  ISBN 0-516-02606-2
  1. Sri Lanka—Juvenile literature. [1. Sri Lanka.]
I. Title. II. Series.
DS489.Z56 1992   91-35252
954.93—dc20   CIP
                                             AC

Picture Acknowledgments
AP/Wide World Photos: 108 (2 photos), 109, 111 (right)
© **Cameramann International, Ltd.:** 18 (2 photos), 30, 38
(right), 48 (right), 63 (left), 65, 68 (bottom), 70 (2 photos),
71 (2 photos), 72 (bottom right), 73 (left), 74 (right), 76
(right), 85 (2 photos), 87 (right), 97 (2 photos), 99 (right),
100, 101 (left), 103, 110, 113

© **Arvind Garg:** 14 (right), 63 (right), 64 (2 photos), 72 (left
and top right), 73 (right), 84 (right)
H. Armstrong Roberts: © **Geopress,** 12, 76 (left), 77;
© **M. Koene,** 47 (left), 52 (left), 57 (right), 68 (top);
© **M. Thonig,** 79
Impact Visuals: © **Arvind Garg,** 52 (right)
North Wind Picture Archives: 23, 38 (left), 42 (2 photos)
Odyssey/Frerck/Chicago: © **Robert Frerck,** 5, 8 (bottom),
13, 21, 27, 28, 29 (2 photos), 41 (right), 47 (right), 48 (left),
49, 54 (2 photos), 61, 81, 87 (left and center), 90 (right)
Photri: 6, 8 (top), 78, 99 (left)
Root Resources: © **Lawrence S. Burr,** 11, 60, 74 (left), 94;
© **B. Crader,** 67
Tom Stack & Associates © **Dave Watts,** 17 (left)
SuperStock International, Inc.: © **Hubertus Kanus,** 15, 91;
© **Shostal Associates, cover inset,** 17 (right), 80; © **Steve
Vidler, Cover,** 20, 82, 89 (left), 92; © **Marie Mattson,** 90
(left); © **Ping Amranand,** 101 (right), 110 (inset)
TSW-CLICK/Chicago: 41 (left), 111 (left); © **Dorothy
Fields,** 16 (left); © **Robert Frerck,** 32, 89 (right), 92 (inset)
Valan: © **Christine Osborne,** 4, 14 (left), 51, 57 (right), 75;
© **K. Ghani,** 16 (right); © **Dr. A. Farquhar,** 84 (left)
Len W. Meents: Maps on 69, 77, 80, 91
**Courtesy Flag Research Center, Winchester,
Massachusetts 01890:** Flag on page 6 (inset) and back
cover
Cover: Tea harvest
Cover Inset: Hand-carved masks

Children walking across a planted rice field

TABLE OF CONTENTS

Sri Lanka has miles of beautiful beaches.
Inset: The Sri Lankan flag

Chapter 1

A SMALL ISLAND COUNTRY

INTRODUCTION

Sri Lanka, once called Ceylon, is a small island country hanging like a gem or a teardrop off the southern coast of India. It has been famous for centuries for its gems, pearls, spices, and tea. In the last fifty years it has gained fame among tourists traveling to Asia. Few other places have so many miles of unspoiled beaches, green mountain scenery of unsurpassed beauty, and exotic festivals.

This little country is also special because of the many different religions and cultures that have lived here for centuries. The two predominant groups are those who speak Sinhalese, who are mostly Buddhists, and those who speak Tamil, who are mostly Hindu. The Sri Lankan flag reflects this diversity. In the center is a yellow lion on a red background symbolizing the Sinhalese people. Around the red rectangle lies a yellow frame representing the Buddhists. A saffron stripe stands for the Hindu people and a green stripe represents the Muslims, who follow Islam.

Sri Lanka has been heavily influenced by its giant neighbor, India. But because it is an island, it has been able to develop a separate identity. For fourteen centuries it was ruled by its own Sinhalese kings. During that period Buddhism and Hinduism

Hills and mountains are found in the center of Sri Lanka.
Rivers (above) run down the hills, through the valleys,
and to the sea. Rice is grown (below) on terraced hillsides.

became an inseparable part of the island's culture. Then various Europeans ruled, some leaving their mark, until Sri Lanka gained its independence in 1948. Since independence, Sri Lanka has struggled to build up its economy, to provide social services to its people, and to resolve a bloody civil war.

RELIEF

The physical characteristics of Sri Lanka are relatively simple. It covers an area of 25,333 square miles (65,610 square kilometers). This is similar in size to the islands of Ireland and Tasmania and slightly larger than the state of West Virginia. It is separated from the Indian peninsula by the Palk Strait, which, at its narrowest point, is only 25 miles (40 kilometers) wide. To the west, south, and east lie thousands of miles of Indian Ocean. In fact, south of Sri Lanka there is no land until one reaches Antarctica.

In the center rises a complex mass of mountains and hills. Between these hills and the coast lie lowlands that constitute four-fifths of the island. Off the coast are coral reefs and unusually deep ocean waters, except at the Palk Strait. The rivers begin in the mountainous center and flow radially outward across the plains to the sea, like the spokes of a wheel.

With the exception of the Jaffna Peninsula, Sri Lanka's rocks are gneiss and granite. These are very hard rocks formed millions of years ago from cooling lava. It is for its gems that the island gained fame. The gems have been mined for centuries in an area on the southwest side near Ratnapura. Probably nowhere else in the world are so many precious and semiprecious stones found in such a small area. Important types are blue sapphires, moonstones, garnets, and zircons.

Other important mineral resources are graphite, of which Sri Lanka was the largest producer in the world for many years, and a good clay for making pottery. Plenty of limestone exists at the Jaffna Peninsula making cement production very plentiful. However, certain limestone areas as well as parts of the coral reefs have been badly damaged by the extraction of lime to be used in mortar. Unfortunately, those resources most important for industry such as coal, iron, and oil have not been found on Sri Lanka and must be imported.

CLIMATE

Sri Lanka's climate is typical of the tropics. The temperature is warm all year round, the yearly average being 80 to 83 degrees Fahrenheit (26.6 to 28.3 degrees Celsius). Up in the mountains it may descend to 60 degrees Fahrenheit (15.5 degrees Celsius), but this is not common elsewhere. Fortunately the heat is bearable in many places, thanks to sea breezes that blow inland. The humidity is also high. Clothing may feel damp and mildew may ruin stored articles.

The four seasons do not exist in Sri Lanka. As in other tropical countries, climatic differences are those between wet and dry seasons, not warm and cold. The wet season is caused by wet winds that blow across the land. The monsoons, as these winds are called, reach Sri Lanka from two different directions and during two different times of the year. The southwest monsoon blows from May to September. It drenches the southwest coast and the hill country. Between November and January a drier monsoon blows from the northeast, bringing rain to the eastern and northern parts of the country. Because the monsoon winds

A reservoir near Sigiriya

are weak, there is very little wind in Sri Lanka. Rain is heavy when it falls, and thunderstorms are common. Though there may be large clouds during part of the day, the nights are clear.

The direction of the monsoons and the different amounts of moisture they carry have divided the island into two parts. The southwest and central hill country are the wet zone, receiving 100 inches (254 centimeters) or more of rain annually. The north half of Sri Lanka together with the east and southeast form the dry zone where rainfall is between 50 and 75 inches (127 and 190.5 centimeters) annually. The dry zone not only gets less rainfall, but the amount of evaporation also is much greater. The rain that does fall returns rapidly to the atmosphere. This has forced the people there to build reservoirs and irrigation channels in order to develop agriculture. This division of the island has had a decisive impact on its history, economy, society, and population distribution.

A fisherman in Trincomalee

REGIONS

The coastal plain, about five to twenty-five miles (eight to forty kilometers) wide, surrounds Sri Lanka like a thin ribbon. Beautiful sandy beaches stretch for miles and behind them stand coconut and palmyra palm trees. In certain sections there are lagoons. Natural rock harbors also occur. The one at Trincomalee is exceptionally attractive and is big and deep enough to hold an entire fleet of modern warships. The soil along the coastal plain tends to be sandy and salty.

Most of the island is made up of rolling plains. In the north the plain is very flat and relatively unpopulated. The Jaffna Peninsula, however, is densely populated with Tamils who cultivate every square inch with tobacco and coconuts. In the southwest the plain has long parallel ridges between which rice is grown in the fertile soil. The southeast, also thinly populated, is mostly forest and areas of scattered trees.

Sunrise from Adam's Peak, which is more than 7,000 feet (more than 2,000 meters) high

Lastly, there is the hill country of the south central region. It is a series of plateaus, hills, and mountains that rise up abruptly from the surrounding plains. From a distance they look like the walls of a gigantic fortress. At its center are the nearly inaccessible Piduru Ridges whose peaks reach 8,000 feet (2,438 meters) above sea level. Sri Lanka's highest mountain, Pidurutalagala, reaching up 8,281 feet (2,524 meters), is among them. Spreading outward are very high ridges, deep valleys, and important basins and plateaus.

Despite its fortresslike appearance, there are many natural entrances to the hill country. For thousands of years cart tracks and footpaths wound through these gaps among the dense forests. The British built a network of roads and a single rail line into the hill country. Almost all of the rivers start here. As they flow toward the plains they fall over the edges of ridges and plateaus in spectacular waterfalls.

Left: A river becomes a bathtub for an elephant.
Right: A grove of teak trees

RIVERS

The rivers of Sri Lanka are not large, but there are many of them. They are known for their beauty as they flow through the rocky gorges of the hill country and form shallow lakes on the plains. At the coast the wide river mouths form flat plains and deltas.

The rivers are important as a source of fish, but they are too wild or too shallow to be navigable except by small boats. The amount of water they hold changes dramatically with the shifting wet and dry seasons. On the flat plains they sometimes stop moving forward and serious flooding results. There are few natural lakes. In the dry zone the people have had to construct reservoirs as well as long canals to supply themselves with water. The Dutch built 153 miles (246 kilometers) of canals along the western coast to provide inland navigation and to channel off floodwaters around the city of Colombo, the capital.

A fisherman tosses his net into the Mahaweli River.

VEGETATION

The vegetation of the dry zone consists of a sparse cover of trees and shrubs. These trees have small leaves that they shed in the dry season. The highest branches of the tallest trees interweave to create a canopy. The acacia tree is typical. The colors of light green and beige dominate this landscape.

The wet zone, on the other hand, has very tall trees with broad leaves that are present year-round. There is dense undergrowth of vines and creepers. The greenery of this wet tropical forest is broken by magnificent orchids. Ebony, teak, and silk wood are representative tree types.

In the hill country, where temperatures are lower, one can find grasslands, stunted forests, and miles of rhododendrons. The trees are often draped in moss. The total effect, when the mountains and valleys are added, is spectacularly beautiful scenery.

Virtually none of the original vegetation remains. Humans have

Left: Many kinds of monkeys live in Sri Lanka and are found throughout the island.
Above: Painted storks in their nest

left their mark everywhere. In addition, Sri Lanka has suffered in recent years from rapid deforestation. This has been caused by slash-and-burn techniques of agriculture, construction projects, an increase in the number of farms, and illegal logging. In certain places the deforestation has led to erosion of the soil.

FAUNA

Sri Lanka is at the southern end of a principal bird migration route. For this reason birds from all over Asia and Europe can be seen. Butterflies are especially large and beautiful. All kinds of insects abound, some of which spread diseases. The best example is malaria. This disease was carried by the anopheles mosquito until the mosquito was controlled in the 1940s. Insect-carried diseases still make raising livestock very difficult.

A young snake charmer (above) and a handler washing his elephant (left)

Typical small animals are squirrels, many types of monkeys, bats, porcupines, and hares. They must take care not to meet lizards; several types of snakes, including cobras; crocodiles; leopards; and bears. Elephants and water buffalo have been domesticated since early in the island's history and are used as important sources of power. During the period of the Sinhalese kingdoms, it was common for kings to own entire stables of elephants. They were prominent in warfare and at royal ceremonies. Until recently elephants were used to uproot trees when jungles were cleared and for carrying heavy loads. In the colorful processions of today, elephants are a key element.

Just as Sri Lanka's forests are disappearing, several animal species such as the wild elephant and the spotted leopard have been threatened with extinction. Since the 1930s, to help stop the extermination, reserves, national parks, and wildlife sanctuaries have been established. About one-fourth of the island is reserved for one type of wildlife protection or another.

Sri Lanka's population grew very fast in the second half of the twentieth century.

POPULATION

Sri Lanka's population had reached over 16.5 million in 1988. Of these, 22 percent were urban dwellers; the rest, inhabitants of the countryside.

The birth rate per one thousand people was 24.8 in 1984. This is quite high considering the country's resources. A population explosion occurred in the second half of the twentieth century. It is due, primarily, to the overwhelming success of eradicating malaria in the 1940s. The population doubled between 1948 and 1981. The population density is one of the highest in all of Asia. However, the people are not spread evenly throughout the island, but are concentrated along the southwestern edge and in the Jaffna Peninsula. Sri Lanka is unique among developing countries in that it has a greater population growth rate in rural areas than in urban areas.

The increasing population creates strains such as overcrowded classrooms, too few hospital beds, higher unemployment, and greater government spending on social programs. The government attempts to combat this serious problem through its family planning program.

The people in Sri Lanka are better off than people elsewhere in South Asia. Life expectancy for males is the highest among all the countries of this area. Adult literacy also is very high. The number of people who could read and write was 87 percent in 1988, compared with 36 percent in India and 76 percent in China.

Immigration and emigration have not been important enough in the twentieth century to affect the population's size.

Sri Lanka is a multicultural state. The most important group is the Sinhalese who form 74 percent of the population. About seven million of these are low-country Sinhalese who live on the plains, and four million are Kandyan Sinhalese who live in the hill country. The other groups are the Tamils, 18 percent; the Moors, 7 percent; and the very small groups (Eurasians, Burghers, Malays, Pakistanis, Europeans, and Veddahs), 1 percent.

Two of these groups are shrinking. The Indian and Sri Lankan governments have agreed to move hundreds of thousands of Indian Tamils back to India. Quite different is the case of the Burghers, a group descended from intermarriages between Tamils, Sinhalese, Portuguese, and Dutch. Though a tiny group, they were powerful and influential until the 1950s, after the country became independent. Then they lost their privileged position and, since then, many have left to settle in such countries as Canada.

SETTLEMENT

The Jaffna Peninsula is densely populated by Sri Lankan Tamils. This area is crisscrossed by a complex network of roads, some of them quite old. The typical village is not centered around a square or road crossing. Rather, it spreads out in all directions with the

Rice terraces

houses lining the roads. Agriculture depends on wells because water does not stay at the surface.

In the beautiful hill country the Kandyan Sinhalese live in villages. Because of the steepness, they have built terraces down the mountainsides on which they plant their rice. Irrigation channels guide water from one level down to another. In the southeast corner Indian Tamils live and work on the large tea estates.

The low-country Sinhalese are both a rural and an urban people. Their villages are built near good, flat, rice-growing land. Forests nearby provide timber and fuel. In some areas farming by peasants has disappeared as rubber and coconut plantations have been established. Traditionally quite isolated, these villages are rapidly becoming involved with the rest of the country as

Pole-sitting fishermen

communication, transportation, and a modern economy expand.

The Sinhalese fishing villages are commonly a cluster of houses near the beach. Some Sinhalese fish from poles set in the water a short distance offshore.

Sinhalese towns usually developed at river crossings. But the towns that have grown into small cities were the port towns. However, there are very few places for good ports. Large bays are not common in Sri Lanka. Ironically, Trincomalee Bay, the largest bay in Sri Lanka and one of the finest natural harbors in the world, does not have a commercial port on it. The bay is located on the east side of the island, away from the main sea route that travels south of Sri Lanka. Colombo, the main port, is almost totally man-made.

Chapter 2

THE SINHALESE KINGDOMS

BEGINNINGS

Homo sapiens (human beings) probably first arrived in Sri Lanka, from India, about 500,000 B.C. They hunted animals and gathered fruits for thousands of years. Sometime between 15,000 B.C. and 10,000 B.C., they began to collect seeds and plant them in the ground. This planting was done under the influence of ideas spreading outward from southeast Asia. Planting produced more food than could be obtained by gathering berries and fruits. Around 5,000 B.C., humans developed the ability to fashion relatively sophisticated stone tools.

The next major transition in the island's history was the arrival of civilization. Civilization is usually described as that level of social development that includes the use of writing, metal, and wheeled carts, and the erection of monumental structures or buildings. The people in a civilized society are divided into classes, political and religious hierarchies, and specialized full-time occupations. Such a society did not develop in Sri Lanka slowly

over the years. Instead it arrived, around 500 B.C., in the form of a group of people called the Sinhalese. They migrated, not from the closest part of southern India, but from the more advanced plains of the north. They brought with them another typical characteristic of civilization—irrigation—which would prove to be of special importance.

The Sinhalese intermarried extensively with the original inhabitants that they found on the island, called Veddahs. Those few Veddahs who were not assimilated disappeared into the jungles and mountains of the east.

The religion of Buddhism had spread throughout India under the important emperor Asoka. In the second half of the third century B.C., Buddhism was brought to Sri Lanka. According to tradition, this was achieved through the arrival of Asoka's brother or son, Prince Mahinda, who convinced the Sinhalese king to adopt the new religion. The king, in turn, converted everyone living in his kingdom. The Sinhalese people believe that their arrival on the island took place simultaneously with the death of the founder of Buddhism, Siddhartha Gautama. Therefore the

Sinhalese inherited the historical duty of ensuring the survival of Buddhism. Nevertheless, Buddhism was not firmly established until 250 years after the Sinhalese arrived.

Around 300 B.C. the Tamils, of Dravidian or south Indian stock, arrived. They had long been traders traveling between their cities along the coast. It was as traders that the Tamils settled in the northernmost tip of Sri Lanka. Their numbers were reinforced later on by Tamil invaders.

The Tamils practiced not Buddhism but the other great Indian religion, Hinduism. Hinduism, an older religion, arrived in Sri Lanka before Buddhism but it was with the arrival of the Tamils that it became a permanent and strong presence. The Tamils had their own language and their culture was very similar to that of south India. There was no conflict between them and the Sinhalese; the island was multiethnic. But because the Sinhalese were the more numerous and the more important, Sri Lanka society had, and has today, a Sinhalese personality.

THE MAHARAJAS

By the first century B.C. the northern half of the island was completely populated. The Sinhalese were busy creating a flourishing civilization centered around the new capital of Anuradhapura.

Like all kings, the monarchs of the Sinhalese, called *maharajas*, had powers and responsibilities. A king's power was the result of his control of the army. Many people believed that he and the queen had divine powers as well. His wealth came from his subjects who gave him one-tenth of what they grew. They also provided their labor for a specified number of days each year during which they built roads, irrigation works, and other public projects.

The king, his ministers, and the rest of his government were relatively weak. This was because power was based on ownership of land and the nobility and the Buddhist monasteries owned very large areas. In addition, the existence of powerful rivals was so common that rarely did one person rule all of the Sinhalese.

One typical Sinhalese king was King Dutthagamani or Gamni the Enraged. In the second century B.C. south Indian invaders crossed the Palk Strait and began a conquest of Sri Lanka. King Dutthagamani led his army northward and stormed the fortress held by the invaders by using elephants to batter down the gates.

Later, at the Sinhalese capital, King Dutthagamani faced the enemy king alone. Each king was mounted on an elephant. King Dutthagamani speared his opponent to death and his elephant killed the enemy king's elephant. The dead king's body was cremated and buried and a monument was built at the site. Music was forbidden to be played there for seven hundred years.

THE IMPORTANCE OF BUDDHISM

Buddhism had a tremendous impact on every aspect of life. It enriched and developed the Sinhala language. It enriched intellectual life and education through the establishment of monasteries. In the monasteries, schools were set up and books on the religious and political histories of the kingdom were written. Buddhism enriched painting, architecture, and sculpture by encouraging the creation of images of the Buddha and of memorials to him called *dagobas*. These are large mounds of earth, brick, and stone.

At times Hindu kingdoms of south India, such as the Chola, ruled Sri Lanka directly or through a Sinhalese king. However, they generally were respectful of Buddhism. There were Hindu priests called *brahmins* at the court and brahmin rituals were followed. But these priests never gained much influence either among the Sinhalese or the Tamil community of Sri Lanka.

TRADE

As with most islands, trade was very important to Sri Lanka. This was especially true of trade with Sri Lanka's next-door neighbor, south India. Where there is trade there is knowledge of faraway places: by the second century Sri Lanka was well known in the Roman Empire and in China. Three centuries later the island had become famous across several continents as an exceptional source of pearls and precious stones.

The Sinhalese kingdoms even sent ambassadors to China and Arabia, and fleets to Persia, India, and Ethiopia. But this expansion did not last long. The Arabs took control of the trade to the west and the Malays took control of the trade to China.

THE IRRIGATION SYSTEM

When the Sinhalese came from relatively dry northwest India, they brought with them the skills and techniques of irrigation construction. They wished to grow rice, a plant requiring a lot of water, on the northern plain where rainfall is quite irregular. The solution was the creation of a very large, sophisticated irrigation system. It was the rival of any other such project in the world and the foundation upon which Sri Lanka's early economy was based.

Water is essential for growing rice.

Fundamental to the irrigation system were reservoirs called tanks. They could be small pools serving only the needs of a few fields or they could be immense lakes that irrigated miles of land and could supply water for cities. The basic idea behind these tanks was expressed by one king who said, "Let not even a small quantity of water obtained by rain go to the sea without benefiting mankind."

Tank building in Sri Lanka began very early, even before the fourth century. During the golden age of irrigation construction, the seventh century, tanks were built that are still important today. To create a tank a natural depression in the ground was chosen. Then an earthen dam was built at the lower end and huge stones were placed on the dam's inner slope and top for reinforcement. An underground channel in the dam led the water to canals for distribution to the rice fields. The water passing through the channel was regulated by a special valve invented by Sinhalese engineers.

In Anuradhapura, founded in the fourth century B.C., an irrigation system that included reservoirs was part of the city planning.

The canals stretching across Sri Lanka also were built with great care. Their gradients were constructed with the precision needed to ensure that, over great distances, the water kept moving but not too rapidly. At one point the network of canals extended over 250 miles (402 kilometers).

The cultural and artistic excellence reached at the capitals of Anuradhapura and Polonnaruwa would never have been possible without the wealth provided by the irrigation. The kings were well aware of this. One of the first Sinhalese kings built a tank before he built his palace.

A very large tank, still standing, is the Kalawewa Tank. It covers 6,380 acres (2,582 hectares) and has a dam 4 miles (6 kilometers) long and 40 feet (12 meters) high. From it, a canal 54 miles (87 kilometers) long and 40 feet wide carries water to Anuradhapura.

Once built, the irrigation system had to be maintained by the organized effort of thousands of people. The peasants, when

Above: A dagoba at Anuradhapura
Left: Lotus columns at Polonnaruwa

working for the king, were required to dredge the canals, clear weeds, and rebuild or reinforce the embankments. They were directed by officials, led by the inspector of reservoirs, who belonged to a special section of the royal government.

ANURADHAPURA AND POLONNARUWA

Anuradhapura was the first capital of the Sinhalese kings. None of the capitals that followed reached its stature as a cultural and political center. Not only was it the king's residence and seat of government but it was a Buddhist religious center of considerable significance. It housed important relics belonging to, or associated with, the Buddha. As a result it became a place of pilgrimage for Buddhists from all over south and east Asia. Within the city and in the hills nearby lived many Buddhist monks, sometimes as many as fifty thousand. These holy men dedicated themselves to

Ruins at Polonnaruwa

scholarship, the design and construction of monuments, and the preservation of the faith.

At its height the city's stone buildings, including important palaces, covered twenty-five square miles (sixty-four square kilometers). But most buildings in those times were built of clay and wood and these extended even farther. Wide avenues crossed the city. At each intersection there was a platform where monks could stand and preach to the people.

The capital was moved by the south Indian Tamil kingdom of Chola during a major invasion. First they destroyed Anuradhapura. Then they purposely built the new capital near the center of the island at Polonnaruwa. Being farther away from India it was less exposed to the attacks Anuradhapura had suffered repeatedly.

When Sinhalese kings returned to power they restored the damaged monuments and ancient temples of Anuradhapura. But the capital remained at Polonnaruwa. Though it grew it never rivaled what the former capital had once been. Nevertheless, it, too, was an impressive city with many royal palaces, monasteries, shrines, parks, and tanks.

INVOLVEMENT WITH SOUTH INDIA

There were periods of peace, wealth, and tranquillity in Sri Lanka under the stronger Sinhalese rulers. But there were also times when conflict was widespread. Powerful men with their followers would struggle against others, each trying to achieve the right to be king and found a dynasty. Or armies from south India would invade and spread destruction such as the plunder of the capital, Anuradhapura, around 100 B.C.

The Tamils of south India frequently invaded Sri Lanka. They wished to control the island's wealth and people. However, at times Tamil involvement in the island was equally the result of rivalries within the Sinhalese leadership. It was common practice for a rival to hire Tamil mercenaries to come over and, together with Sinhalese rebel soldiers, fight for the throne. If the attempt was successful these foreigners became powerful and the new king owed them gratitude. If they stayed in Sri Lanka they could never be trusted and could cause turmoil within the country.

Between the seventh and eleventh centuries the three Tamil kingdoms of Pandya, Pallava, and Chola ruled in different parts of south India. At times the Sinhalese, as an ally of one of them, would enter south India to attack another Tamil kingdom. If their side was victorious the Sinhalese could share in the spoils.

The rock fortress at Sigiriya was a royal citadel for more than eighteen years in the fifth century. It is 600 feet (183 meters) high and the summit spreads over nearly 3 acres (1.2 hectares).

THE DECLINE OF THE SINHALESE KINGDOMS

Eventually the strife between political or military leaders became chronic and caused permanent damage. General fought general, innumerable rivals for the throne struggled against each other, and armies of south Indian kingdoms joined in when it might be to their advantage.

The central government began to lose control over its territory. As a result, in the fourteenth century, an independent kingdom of Sri Lankan Tamils arose in the northernmost part of the island. With a kingdom of their own, they gained considerable confidence in themselves. Their culture, previously influenced by the

Buddhist Sinhalese, became more similar to the pure Hindu Tamil culture of south India. They also gained control of the famous and valuable pearl fishery. Up until this time it had been an important source of income for the Sinhalese.

The Sinhalese armies that battled each other across the northern plain destroyed the irrigation system that gave life to the people of Sri Lanka. Water no longer reached the rice fields. The farmers turned to slash-and-burn agriculture, which provided only enough food for the farmer and his family. Abandoned canals and tanks, now full of vegetation, became breeding grounds for mosquitoes. These insects spread malaria and therefore death. To escape the famine and the malaria, large numbers of Sinhalese left the dry zone. They migrated to the mountainous center of the island and to the southwest and southeast. This depopulation of the north only hastened the abandonment of sophisticated agriculture.

By the fifteenth century the important Sinhalese kingdoms were gone for good. An independent Sri Lanka was about to disappear for several hundred years. The population of the island as a whole was far below what it had previously been. Since the irrigation system no longer functioned, the Sinhalese had to import their rice. As this period of Sri Lanka's history drew to a close the island became divided into three areas. To the north were the Tamils who looked to south India more than ever. Along the southern coasts the Sinhalese turned to cultivating the wet zone seriously for the first time. And between the two there grew up in the northern plain a vast, uninhabited forest. It would serve to separate the Sinhalese and the Tamils for centuries.

Chapter 3

FOREIGNERS
COME AND GO

It would seem natural that the only foreigners to impose their will on Sri Lanka would have been their neighbors, the Indians. Instead, people from very distant parts of the world and extremely different cultures ruled the Sinhalese for hundred of years. The reasons for this were, in large part, the European interest in buying spices and, later, in controlling nearby India.

THE ARABS

As the Sinhalese gradually shifted their population and kingdoms to the southwest, agriculture declined and the revenues collected by the governments fell. To supplant the lost income, they began exporting two commodities greatly in demand in medieval Europe. These were the spices called cinnamon, which grew wild in the forests of the southwest, and pepper. Both were royal monopolies. Foreign merchants came to Sri Lanka, bought them at prices fixed by the government, and shipped them off. Three southwestern coastal towns, Colombo, Galle, and Negombo, developed into ports of foreign trade. The major international traders were the Arabs and they gradually settled in these ports, beginning in the seventh century.

The Arabs, Muslims by religion, were the first distant foreigners to actually live on the island. Romans, Byzantines, Persians, and Chinese had met in Sri Lanka occasionally, in order to buy and sell silk, but they never settled there. The arrival of the Arabs was to be expected because they had created an extensive shipping network to supply the Europeans with spices. Besides cinnamon and pepper, they exported jewels, pearls, emery, incense, and timber. Unlike the foreigners that followed, they did not get involved in the affairs of the Sinhalese kingdoms.

THE PORTUGUESE

In the thirteenth, fourteenth, and fifteenth centuries, the Europeans, wealthier and more powerful than before, began a series of attacks on the Arabs. They wished to regain lands lost to the Arabs centuries before and to control for themselves the profitable spice trade between Asia and Europe. At first, the people of Portugal were among the most successful in achieving these goals.

The first contact of the Portuguese with the island was by accident. During a battle between Arab and Portuguese ships in 1505 in the Indian Ocean, a Portuguese ship was blown by chance to Sri Lanka. The Portuguese stayed. The Sinhalese could do little about it. The continuing dynastic disputes among the Sinhalese rulers made this certain. Some of them asked the Portuguese to help them defeat threatening rivals to the throne. In return, the Portuguese demanded and received rights to settle in the ports and to control the export trade. But to the north, the kingdom of Jaffna was far more cohesive. The Portuguese found the Tamils violently resistant to losing their independence and did not conquer them until 1591. This brought to an end the last independent Tamil state in Sri Lanka. Portugal's dominance of the seas ensured that no one else would dispute their position in Sri Lanka for some time.

Though always concentrating on increasing their wealth through control of trade, the Portuguese were not satisfied. They were determined to rule the whole island themselves, though indirectly. They also felt it their religious duty to convert the people to Roman Catholicism. For this they brought in missionaries.

The missionaries set up schools where some Sinhalese were taught to read and write in Portuguese, Sinhala, or Tamil. The schools also taught Catholicism and basic European ideas. Intolerant of other religions, the Portuguese destroyed the Buddhist and Hindu temples. Naturally, the Arab traders were ordered to leave and some did. But the Portuguese realized that the Arabs were skilled sailors and traders so that many were allowed to stay unofficially.

Where the Portuguese failed was in their goal to control the entire island. They were already in possession of the coast, also called the low country. Nevertheless, they could not overrun the Sinhalese kingdom of Kandy located in the mountains. They fell victim to the tropical diseases rampant in the jungles. And they did not forget that their main purpose in being in Sri Lanka was to control the trade that flowed through the ports of the coast. Those Sinhalese, such as the Buddhist monks, who fled Portuguese domination found refuge in the kingdom of Kandy.

The Portuguese did not establish their own government in the coastal kingdoms. Instead, except for the Portuguese governor, the local people continued to rule. Following Sinhalese custom, the Portuguese awarded land to Europeans and Sinhalese in return for important services.

Unlike the Arabs before them the Portuguese made a lasting, though minor, impact on Sinhalese society. Many of the more important families of the coast converted to Catholicism, attended the Portuguese schools, and took Portuguese names. They hoped, in this manner, to achieve better relations with the Europeans. Today there are still Catholics on the island though they are a small group. Many of the powerful families among the low-country Sinhalese, though no longer Catholics, still have Portuguese names. Family names like de Silva, de Soysa, Fernando, Perera, and de Mel are found in present-day Sri Lanka.

THE DUTCH

As the Portuguese had taken the Indian Ocean spice trade away from the Arabs, in the seventeenth century the Dutch replaced the Portuguese with their own trading empire in Asia. One result was that they forced the Portuguese out of Sri Lanka. As usual, the Dutch received help from the Sinhalese themselves. The kingdom of Kandy looked for support to oust the Portuguese. Between 1638 and 1658 the Dutch took control of all the coastal areas, including Jaffna.

The Dutch who settled in Sri Lanka lived in the towns though some owned land in the countryside. They built forts in the major ports. Small groups of Portuguese and Muslims were the other foreigners in these towns, the Muslims remaining the chief traders.

The Dutch made profits by exporting cinnamon, pepper, pearls,

Left: The British East India Company had an office building in Amsterdam in the 1600s. Right: The fort at Galle was originally built by the Portuguese and the Dutch added to it.

gems, and two hundred elephants a year. They imported tea, silk, sugarcane, porcelain, copper, and iron. Some made large sums of money by operating taverns that sold an alcoholic beverage called *toddy*.

Like the Portuguese, the Dutch were more interested in making money than in ruling the local people. They left administration of the low-country Sri Lanka basically in the hands of the Sinhalese and Tamils. They, too, could not resist attempts to conquer Kandy, but their expeditions into the mountains always ended in failure.

A major transformation brought about by the Dutch was the establishment of plantations. These very large farms, worked by hired labor and growing a single crop over a large area, were in the coastal lowlands. On them the Dutch grew cinnamon, and later, coffee, sugarcane, coconuts, cotton, tobacco, and rice. The rice was grown to decrease the amount of rice that was imported. But the rest were cash crops, that is, agricultural products that were not consumed by the local people but were sold to other countries in order to make a profit. Under the Dutch, and later the British, the plantations, not the farmers, came to provide the bulk of the government's revenues.

The other major contribution of the Dutch was the reform of the judicial system. The Dutch carefully organized the laws and customs of the Tamils and the Muslims for the first time. They applied their own Dutch law to the Sinhalese. In each of the provinces they established a central court. Dutch law is still an important part of the Sri Lankan legal system today.

The Dutch continued the efforts of the Portuguese to provide a European education to some of the people. These schools, over many years, led to a split among the Sinhalese. Some of the Tamils and low-country Sinhalese became familiar with, and sometimes appreciated, European customs, ideas, and languages. But the Kandyan Sinhalese, unaffected by these educational efforts, remained ignorant of foreign cultures. As for religion, the Dutch made virtually no effort to convert anyone to their beliefs.

THE BRITISH

By the end of the eighteenth century, a new group of Europeans, the British, were creating an empire that stretched around the globe. However, the Indian Ocean spice trade had become a thing of the past and cinnamon had lost most of its former importance. Rather than being a source of wealth to those who controlled it, Sri Lanka had become a colony that was expensive to keep.

So when the British East India Company, a private trading firm, was attracted to Sri Lanka, it was not with the idea of making money. The company controlled valuable ports along the east coast of India, which occasionally suffered from the monsoon winds. They searched for a place that would be big enough to shelter the naval fleet that protected their Indian ports from French attacks.

They found what they desired at Trincomalee on Sri Lanka's east coast. With the intention of taking it for themselves, the British company defeated the Dutch in 1796. While the Sinhalese and the Tamils watched, they took over all of lowland Sri Lanka. In 1802, the island became the first British crown colony and they officially called it Ceylon. In a crown colony the people did not participate in governing their land to the extent found in other British colonies.

The British were the first to place the entire island under a single ruler; unfortunately for the Sinhalese—a foreign ruler. As had the Portuguese and Dutch, the British sent expeditions against Kandy but the difficult terrain and the tropical diseases defeated them at first. The situation changed when they built roads into the mountainous countryside. This made it difficult for the Kandyan soldiers to practice the guerrilla warfare they had used successfully for centuries.

Another reason for Britain's victory was disunity among the Kandyans. Sinhalese nobles were unhappy with the king who was of Tamil descent. In 1815 they invited the British to throw him off the throne. The British sent the king and all his family into permanent exile in south India, and united the kingdom with the rest of Sri Lanka as the Crown Colony of Ceylon.

Soon after their arrival in Kandy, the British wrote lengthy

The Buddhist perahera festival (above) and a Hindu festival (right) are only two of the many festivals celebrated today in Kandy.

descriptions of life in this part of the island, untouched by foreigners. They found a country that was marked by poverty. The people grew only rice, but since they did not grow enough to feed everyone extra quantities had to be imported. The peasants paid taxes to their governors in the form of rice at harvest time. Social differences were very important. The royal family and the governors kept themselves as distant as possible from the common people. Despite the country's lack of wealth, the king was surrounded by a very large court. For example, the attention the king required just for his bath and personal care was provided by over five hundred nobles. Poor and rich alike celebrated four great festivals each year with a large and colorful parade in the capital. Buddhism was the only religion practiced in Kandy.

The British brought Tamils from south India to work in the tea industry about 1900. They were employed to pick the green leaves (left) and grade and sort the dried leaves (right).

CHANGES BROUGHT BY THE BRITISH

The British brought more economic, political, social, and cultural changes than any of the other foreigners. Many of these changes were the result of efforts to keep the cost of ruling Sri Lanka as low as possible. One measure taken was the creation of a new bureaucracy, the Ceylon Civil Service. The British created a bureaucracy to run the colony. It was made up of British and trained Sinhalese. The Sinhalese were paid less than the British. Land was sold to Europeans who were willing to cultivate it. A special effort was made to increase coffee production. For example, the tax on coffee was less than on other export crops, and a special bank, the Ceylon Bank, was opened to help establish coffee plantations.

When the price of coffee on the world market fell, the planters found new success with tea. Beginning around 1870 it became Sri Lanka's major export. Unfortunately for the people, the British paid so much attention to their plantations that very little thought was spent on the rest of the country. A significant road and rail system was constructed to serve the plantations. Nothing was done to increase rice production, so large quantities were imported from British India.

To work on the coffee and tea plantations, the British brought in Tamils from south India. They lived in the central highlands surrounded by Buddhist Sinhalese. Another group that developed at this time were those low-country Sinhalese and Tamils who gained power through having a British education and holding positions in the civil service bureaucracy or participating in the export economy.

INDEPENDENCE

As elsewhere in the world, nationalism—the desire of a group of people to rule themselves—arrived in Sri Lanka. It developed in the island during the last three decades of the nineteenth century. The Sinhalese, the most nationalistic ethnic group, expressed this desire through their efforts to keep their religion, Buddhism, strong. However, as the British transferred more and more power to the Sinhalese bureaucrats, the minority groups, led by the Sri Lankan Tamils, became alarmed. They feared independence would lead to discrimination against them.

With their new power, the important Sinhalese government officials began to make fundamental changes. For the first time in centuries, a serious program to restore the irrigation works in the dry zone was begun. Education, health services, and food were made available at much cheaper prices.

During the 1930s and 1940s nationalists in India convinced the

British that they would have to give their South Asian colonies complete independence very soon. But the start of World War II halted all political change. The British concentrated on defending themselves from the Japanese. In April of 1942 the Japanese attacked Sri Lanka in an effort to eliminate the naval bases at Trincomalee and Colombo. Over one thousand Allied troops and Sri Lankan civilians died.

Three years after the end of World War II, on February 4, 1948, the British colony of Ceylon regained its independence. Unlike the terrible ethnic violence that killed millions when India and Burma gained their freedom, Sri Lanka's first years were tranquil.

The first government of independent Sri Lanka was fortunate. Rubber and tea brought in high prices and the profits were used to create programs in education, health, and housing. The government also tried to reduce the island's dependence on imported rice by beginning a long-term project to increase irrigated farmland.

A new government, elected in 1956, had more popular backing than the previous one. But it favored the Sinhalese and Buddhists over other groups and this increased tension. In the 1970s unemployment rose, as did prices, and important consumer goods became more scarce. Many of the plantations and foreign-owned factories were taken over by the government.

Especially troubling was the new attitude of the Tamil minority. Tired of being ignored, and losing jobs and possibilities of getting a good education, they gave up their demand for participation in Sri Lanka's government and insisted instead on creating a separate Tamil country. Young Tamils turned to terrorist tactics and violence between Sinhalese and Tamils increased. Through all of this Sri Lanka has continued to be a democratic country, but the island is no longer at peace with itself.

Chapter 4

RELIGION

Reflecting a history filled with the arrivals of very different peoples, Sri Lanka is a country with many religions. The four main religions of the world are represented, though not in equal numbers. Sixty-nine percent of the population is Buddhist; 15 percent, Hindu; 8 percent, Muslim; and 8 percent, Christian.

Two of these religions, Buddhism and Hinduism, are South Asian religions. They are very different from Christianity and Islam, which developed in the Middle East. Both Asian religions stress the idea that the material or real world that we experience around us is false. What is real is a special type of knowledge that can be achieved only after much effort. Also fundamental is the idea that everything is cyclical, everything repeats itself, even people are reborn after they die.

BUDDHISM

Buddhism has always been of great importance in Sri Lanka because it is the religion of the majority Sinhalese. The Sinhalese kings gave Buddhism their official protection for many centuries.

With the arrival of the foreigners it lost its preferred status. Today Buddhism is still a significant force in politics and society. The 1978 constitution states that Buddhism is the most important religion, but that freedom of religion is to be allowed for all.

Buddhism was founded by Siddhartha Gautama in the sixth century B.C. He was a wealthy prince who lived comfortably in the Himalayan foothills of northern India. He was shocked one day when he saw an old man and later when he saw a sick man and a corpse—things he had not been allowed to see before. At the age of twenty-nine he gave up his wealth and spent five years searching for the way to conquer sorrow, sickness, and death. Finally, after intense meditation under a tree, he envisioned what became the main beliefs of his religion. Because of his wisdom he came to be known by the title of the *Buddha*, which means the "Wise One" or "Enlightened One."

To his followers he preached the essential Four Noble Truths. The first is that sorrow and pain make up most of human existence. Secondly, the source of sorrow is desire and attachment. Thirdly, and logically, if desire ceases, so will sorrow. And, lastly, desire is halted by separating one's self from the world, from one's senses, and from one's self. When the believer no longer wants anything, it will become clear to that person that there is nothing permanent in the world. He or she will also realize that individual human beings are totally unimportant.

The Buddha recognized the existence of gods, but he claimed that none of them were all-powerful and eternal. He did not explain how the world was created. The Buddhist does not require the activity of priests or participation in ceremonies in order to reach salvation. Meditation is sufficient.

After the Buddha's death, his teachings and sayings were

A shrine (above) in front of a bo tree that is more than two thousand years old. Buddhists (left) sit before a gigantic statue of Buddha.

written down. The religion also broke into several subgroups. Almost all Sri Lankan Buddhists belong to the Theravada branch. They believe in following the Buddha's ideas strictly and they emphasize individual salvation. In other parts of Asia, the Mahayana branch predominates. It stresses giving attention to *bodhisattvas*, who are somewhat like saints and help other individuals gain salvation.

At the time Buddhism arrived in Sri Lanka, it was accompanied by sacred relics that became of great importance to the Sinhalese. The Buddha's right collarbone and his alms bowl are two examples. A major relic is the bo, or bodhi, tree in Anuradhapura. The Buddha reached enlightenment while meditating under a bo tree. The original, in India, no longer exists, but a cutting was brought to the island and planted. The tree that grew from that cutting still stands, an object of special reverence. However, the most sacred of all is the Buddha's right eyetooth. No Sinhalese king, it was believed, had the right to rule unless he had the tooth

Inside the Temple of the Tooth in Kandy (above), the tooth relic is kept in seven jeweled gold caskets (right).

relic. Over the years it came to symbolize the strength and independence of the Sinhalese people. It is kept in the Temple of the Tooth in Kandy.

The only true Buddhist is the person who dedicates his or her entire life to following the teaching of the Buddha. The goal to be reached is perfect understanding or knowledge. This brings release from the seemingly endless cycle of rebirths to which all lesser humans are subjected. Men who attempt to do this are called monks and either wander or live in monasteries. Women may become nuns. A particular group of Buddhist monks is called a *sangha*. They take vows of poverty, of chastity, and to harm no living thing. Since they do not work, they beg from local villagers. By filling the monk's bowl with rice, villagers gain religious merit. The monasteries were the single, most important institution in Sri Lanka before the arrival of the foreigners. They controlled education, advised the king, and owned vast tracts of land.

48

A group of young Buddhist monks

Buddhism does not provide guidance to the common man or woman who wishes to get divine help to solve life's everyday problems. So popular Buddhism includes worshiping a large number of local, regional, and national gods. Before Buddhism existed these gods were worshiped as animist spirits or Hindu gods. The Buddha himself has been transformed into a god by the common people. He is the most important of the gods and is believed to be present in his relics. All other gods have humanlike personalities and weaknesses. Gods worshiped by Buddhists include Saman, Vishnu, Skanda, Pattini, and Natha. Worshipers show their reverence with offerings of flowers and vegetables. Below the gods are local demons and ghosts and spirits and goblins representing the forces of evil. Though it has nothing to do with Buddhism, most Sinhalese also are faithful followers of astrology.

Buddhism is what has given Sri Lanka its specialness—its

identity. Buddhism disappeared from India after the Buddha's death. The Sinhalese believe they were chosen by the Buddha to preserve Buddhism in South Asia.

In the twentieth century, Buddhism has experienced a revival. It was instrumental in the efforts of the Sinhalese to gain independence and live their lives without foreign pressure. The monks have considerable influence, even in elections. But the modern world has brought crisis as well. Many monks are moving from the hills around Kandy, where they traditionally lived, to settle in cities. Temple lands are much reduced. As village life loses its traditional character, there are fewer peasants to fill the alms bowls. In the cities the monks are enrolling in universities. Some are entering professions or taking jobs that contradict their intention of isolating themselves from society and the material world.

HINDUISM

Like Buddhism, Hinduism spread from India to Sri Lanka. Unlike Buddhism, Hinduism has no founder. It is a religion that evolved out of ancient beliefs and traditions over thousands of years. The beliefs and traditions have been preserved in the sacred scriptures called the Vedas. Hinduism in Sri Lanka is the religion of the Sri Lankan Tamils and of the Indian Tamils.

The most important spiritual being is Brahman, the universal soul. Below is a trinity of the most important gods: Brahma the Creator, Vishnu the Preserver, and Siva the Destroyer. Each one takes on many different names and forms. Many Hindus are followers of either Vishnu or, as in Sri Lanka, Siva.

Sri Lankan Hindus are devoted to Siva the Destroyer. This is

Representations of the elephant-headed Ganesha and brahmin priests

not because they believe in destruction, but because they respect the force of change in life. They worship Siva in the form of Nataraja, Lord of the Dances. He is shown having several arms and dancing before a circle of flames. The dancing represents the rhythm of the universe, the numerous arms represent Siva's different powers, and the circle of flames symbolizes the cyclical nature of the universe.

Other popular Hindu gods in Sri Lanka are Parvati, Siva's wife and the goddess of fertility, and their two sons, elephant-headed Ganesha and Skanda—often thought of as a god of war. Sri Lanka's Hindus celebrate over thirty festivals each year.

Hindu worship consists of treating a god as one would an honored guest: offering food, water, flowers, and incense. Music and dancing also are provided to entertain the gods. Priests are in charge of worship. As in Buddhism, Hindus worship as individuals, not as a congregation. Rituals also are performed by the family in the home.

Above: Muslim students
Left: A Hindu temple in Trincomalee

Hindus believe that no living being should be harmed. Not surprising, vegetarianism is very common. All Hindus also accept the caste system. This means that humans are categorized by the occupational group into which they are born. Castes are ranked in order of their ritual purity or religious value. Members of the higher castes follow Hindu practices more strictly than those of lower castes. Hindu temples have priests of the same caste as the worshipers.

ISLAM

Islam was born in the Middle East, an area with a cultural and physical atmosphere very different from South Asia. It arrived in Sri Lanka with the Arab traders who settled there in the seventh century. It continues to be practiced by a minority of Sri Lankans.

Islam's central belief is expressed as, "There is no God but Allah (God); and Muhammad is His prophet." In other words, worship of any god other than Allah is totally unacceptable. Muhammad, Islam's founder in the seventh century A.D., is believed to be the most important prophet to have lived. Muhammad's words are written in the holy book called the Quran. However, Muhammad is never prayed to as God or as any other type of spiritual being.

The basic requirements of Islam are repetition of the central beliefs, almsgiving, fasting during the holy month of Ramadan, and, if possible, a pilgrimage to the holy city of Mecca in Saudi Arabia.

Islam in Sri Lanka has been influenced by local customs. For example, the Muslim tradition that the two sexes have very limited contact with each other is not strictly followed. Another special characteristic of the Sri Lankan Muslim community is its inclusion of the Hindu wedding ceremony in the traditional Islamic wedding.

CHRISTIANITY

The majority of Christians in Sri Lanka are Roman Catholics. The Catholics are concentrated along the west coast. Their prominence along this coast is thought to be the result of the success of the Portuguese among the fisherman caste. This caste occupies a relatively low position in the caste system. On becoming Catholics they could reject the whole idea of the caste system and their place in it.

Sri Lankan Catholics have certain unique characteristics. Perhaps the most interesting are the Passion Plays of Holy Week that include Tamil and Sinhalese songs and dances.

Pilgrims and tourists climb Adam's Peak (left) to see "Buddha's footprint" at the top (above).

SRI LANKA: A MULTIFAITH STATE

Today there is no official religion in Sri Lanka. Freedom of worship is observed. The holy days of all four religions are officially recognized as national holidays. The 1978 constitution does recognize, however, the special importance of Buddhism.

An excellent symbol of the country's multifaith nature is the mountain in the southwest called Adam's Peak. At the top is an indentation in the shape of a footprint. Before any of the major religions arrived it was possibly the center of a cult that worshiped a mountain god. Today, the Buddhists believe that it is the sacred footprint made by the Buddha during a visit. Hindus believe it was the god Siva who made the mark. And Muslims believe that Adam, after his expulsion from the Garden of Eden, was forced to stand with one foot on top of this mountain as further punishment. Pilgrims of all three religions climb the mountain once a year.

Chapter 5

THE PEOPLE AND EVERYDAY LIFE

Virtually everyone in Sri Lanka has the same physical appearance. Yet linguistic and religious differences divide people to an astounding extent. The Sinhalese, the Tamils, and the Burghers are identified primarily by the language each one speaks. It is language that causes most of the friction between groups in Sri Lanka. Four major religions are represented on the island: Buddhism, Hinduism, Islam, and Christianity.

But differences go deeper than language and religion. The Sinhalese and the Tamils, for example, are organized according to the rigid caste system. Muslims and Burghers are not. All of these groups are concentrated in particular geographic areas. As a result, it is normal to live in an area or city in which most people speak the same language, worship in the same way, and share the same culture. There is very little intermarriage between the main groups. Membership in an ethnic group provides a person with his or her principal identity in life. People's loyalty to their group is far and above any patriotic feelings toward Sri Lanka.

Sri Lanka is a developing nation with extremes in income and living standards. These differences can be seen between social classes and between rural and urban people. The great majority of the people are relatively poor. There is a minority that is very wealthy and a minority that is middle class.

In the past fifty years, Sri Lanka has been flooded with Western culture. Before World War II, knowledge of European ideas and culture was limited to a small elite group living in or near Colombo. But today, blue jeans and Coca-Cola, bikini-clad tourists, and Japanese microbuses can be seen everywhere. A balance has been reached between traditional culture and the new, foreign ways. The two exist comfortably together in clothing, house furnishings, use of leisure time, the selection and preparation of foods, medicine, and attitudes toward employment, health, and education.

THE SINHALESE

The Sinhalese are the largest ethnic and linguistic group. They are Buddhists and believe that their particular form of Buddhism is purer than all others. They are divided into two groups. The low-country Sinhalese live in the south and western coastal region. The Kandyan Sinhalese, a slightly smaller group, live in the south central highlands. The first group of Sinhalese have had contact with foreigners for centuries but the Kandyans have been in touch with the outside world only since the nineteenth century, which gives them a more old-fashioned outlook. Most Sinhalese are farmers, living in villages where rice growing is the main occupation. Their social organization is the caste system.

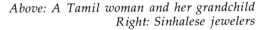

Above: A Tamil woman and her grandchild
Right: Sinhalese jewelers

THE TAMILS

The Tamils are the second-largest ethnic group and are followers of Hinduism. Their language, Tamil, is spoken by millions of people in nearby southern India. They too follow the caste system.

Despite sharing a common religion, culture, and language, the Tamils of Sri Lanka are divided into two relatively distinct groups. Those living along the coasts of the north and east—about half the Tamil population—have been living on the island for at least a thousand years. They are hardworking farmers who cultivate the least fertile part of the country. Perhaps because of the limitations imposed by the land, Sri Lankan Tamils, as they are called, have always jumped at the opportunity to get a formal education. One outcome of this interest is that the number of Sri Lankan Tamils holding positions in the government is far out of proportion to their numbers in the country's population.

The Indian Tamils are relatively recent arrivals: they were brought to the island from India by the British in the nineteenth and early twentieth centuries. In India they were one of the poorest and most illiterate groups. In Sri Lanka they were settled in the central highlands as workers on the tea-growing estates. Living at a distance from the Sri Lankan Tamils and surrounded by the very different Sinhalese, they remained totally isolated from the country's population and kept close ties, instead, with south India. Until recently everyone else considered them foreigners. Even the Sri Lankan Tamils looked down on them because the Indian Tamils belong to a much lower caste and because their educational level is far inferior.

OTHER ETHNIC GROUPS

Living mostly along the coasts, the Muslims are urban dwellers. In Sri Lanka they are usually called Moors—the name given to people of northwest Africa. (The Portuguese had the erroneous habit of calling any Muslim a Moor and the name has stuck.) The Muslims of Sri Lanka speak Tamil but are very different from the Tamils in culture and, of course, religion. They work in the towns and cities as traders, small-scale merchants, and shopkeepers.

A small but interesting group are the Burghers. This term applies to people of European ancestry, mainly Dutch and Portuguese. Some look European but others are of mixed race. They use English as their main language though they are fluent in other languages as well. The Burghers are either Catholics or Protestants, highly educated, and mainly an urban people. Under the British, they dominated the government bureaucracy, the professions, and trade. For such a small group of people, they held a vast amount of power. However, since independence and the rise of Sinhalese and Tamil nationalism, they have lost their dominant position. Many have left Sri Lanka to live in Great Britain, Australia, New Zealand, and Canada.

The Veddahs are the original inhabitants of the island. Over the centuries they have isolated themselves from the other groups that settled in Sri Lanka. But, like other aboriginal peoples of the world (such as the Aborigines of Australia), their days are numbered. Originally they lived a primitive life-style. They were hunters and gatherers. Or they used a primitive form of agriculture involving the burning of forests to clear temporary plots for planting. They lived in simple villages. But as other groups have spread throughout the island and the government has become more organized, their culture has been weakened. They are being absorbed into the larger and more powerful communities around them. Some anthropologists believe that today no one can be found who fluently speaks the Veddah language. Their existence also is threatened by the new national parks. The Veddahs cannot burn forests in these areas. Laws against hunting in these parks protect endangered wildlife, but also end one of the Veddahs' principal means of surviving. In 1970 it was estimated that several thousand Veddahs still lived as they had for so many centuries. In the 1980s they numbered only a few hundred.

THE CASTE SYSTEM

Both the Sinhalese and Tamil societies are organized according to the caste system. A caste governs a group of families and its

Women from a fishing village

specific relationships with other groups of families in the same area. The caste system is supported by religion because Hinduism and Buddhism (only in Sri Lanka) teach that different castes are connected to different levels of religious purity. In other words, the people of the lowest castes are the least pure while those in the high castes are exceptionally pure.

Caste influences a person's life from the smallest details to the most important issues. Each caste is traditionally associated with a specific trade or occupation so that those belonging to a certain caste usually follow the occupation of that caste, for example farming. Castes are closed: one is born into caste and no matter how one's life as an individual may change, one will die a member of that caste. Similarly, people only marry within their caste.

Sri Lanka is unique in that the Sinhalese are the only Buddhists in the world who accept the caste system. The dominant caste is that of the farmers. Ranked below them are the craftsmen,

Water buffalo are used as work animals.

barbers, fishermen, laundrymen, and others. The government does not recognize the existence of the caste system.

In the cities and especially in Colombo, the caste system has been weakening. Modern employment practices there require a more flexible social order that places emphasis on an individual's skills, experience, or education.

These changes have affected the so-called untouchables especially. These are people who are religiously so impure that, by tradition, contact with them is avoided by members of other castes. With the backing of the government, and after several riots, the untouchables have gained entrance to some temples and the right to be served by barbers and at restaurants.

RURAL LIFE

It is in the countryside that the traditional way of life continues much as it has for hundreds of years. At its center is the village or town and the farming communities that live there. Surrounded by rice fields or by forests, or at a junction of country roads, the typical village is a collection of small houses set among trees. The air is usually filled with the sounds of yapping dogs, cackling hens, and the cries of small children. Each house has a garden containing frangipani trees with their brilliant red flowers, orchids, hens, a small dog, a cat, and perhaps a mynah bird or parrot.

In the villagers' daily lives, the most important building is the general store that sells bread, sugar, tea, soup, cigars, oil lamps, and so forth. The villagers pay for these goods with credit until after the harvest. One can buy city newspapers and listen to the radio, which is left on for most of the day in the general store. Men visit the store to drink tea and talk. If a discussion turns into a quarrel there may eventually be a lawsuit. Sri Lankan villagers are fascinated by trials and will go into debt to hire a lawyer to defend them on some unimportant matter. For items not carried by the general store, there is the weekly market. On market day people gather at the marketplace to trade their farm products for utensils, cloth, toys, and plastic products.

Everyone works except the very young, the very old, and the sick. In the fields men wear a white cotton loincloth called a *lungi* or a *sarong*, a skirt formed from a long cotton or silk strip loosely wrapped around the waist and tucked in. Women wear the *sari*, a long strip of cloth wound around the body. There is a barber, a wood and metal craftsman, and a school that is simply a cleared space with a roof over it to keep out the rain and sun. Washing is done on the edge of streams by the washer caste. There also is a shop specializing in *ayurvedic* medicine—a form of ancient medicine based on herbal remedies. If the village is large enough, there will be a government-run pharmacy.

A village council, together with the village headman, keeps order and coordinates group efforts. Fathers are the respected and revered heads of family. A father's most important responsibility

In the countryside each house has a garden (left) and clothes are washed at the edge of the river (right).

is to plan the marriages of his children. Intermarriage within a group of families, or caste, is common. Weddings are the gayest events in the village. But no one is wealthy enough to go on a honeymoon. Today there are relatively few young, single adults in the villages. Many move to the city to find employment and a more exciting life-style.

Both men and women chew betel, a mixture of betel leaves, areca nuts, and lime. It leaves a very noticeable red stain in the mouth and on the teeth. Both sexes smoke small cigars. The men also smoke cigarettes. The alcoholic drink most often consumed is toddy, which is made from the juice of the flowers of several kinds of palm trees. Tea is very popular.

HEALTH AND EDUCATION

In a hot and humid tropical country like Sri Lanka, where religious traditions are often opposed to scientific medical thinking, keeping the people healthy is a challenge. Sri Lanka was

Rural schoolchildren (left) and the University of Peradeniya (right)

one of the first developing countries to eradicate malaria, which is spread by mosquitoes, and tuberculosis. The campaign against malaria in the 1940s was so successful that the population has increased dramatically ever since.

In Sri Lanka the government pays for everyone's medical needs. The number and quality of the hospitals are better than average. Rural health centers have been built to care for infants and their mothers. Nevertheless, there is an acute shortage of doctors. Sri Lankan students avoid medical studies and choose, overwhelmingly, the easier education and career of a government office worker. Hospitals are overcrowded. In the countryside health education is a priority to fight contaminated food and water.

Education from grade school to university is free. Because the government has invested so heavily in education, the literacy rate is very high: 87 percent in 1988. The great majority of schools and colleges are owned and run by the government. In the universities, few students are interested in taking vocational or technical courses because manual labor is associated with low-

Only the main rail lines are now in service.

caste occupations. Such disdain will cause problems for society and has already led to violent behavior by university graduates who cannot find employment.

TRANSPORTATION

Rail transportation in Sri Lanka goes back to the British. They built the first rail line. Eventually the rail network covered the entire country and tied it together better than any other form of transport. Over the years many lines have been abandoned and only the main trunk lines still are in service. Colombo is the center of rail transportation. The rail line to Talaimannar in the north connects to the ferry that runs between Sri Lanka and India.

Road transport is an astonishing world of its own. All sorts of vehicles can be found, often all at the same time, filling the city streets: cars, bullock carts, bicycles, trucks, and buses. Pedestrians fill the spaces in between. Driving in the countryside is a death-defying sport by Western standards because the narrow, winding roads are often occupied, unexpectedly, with children, cattle, bicycles, and speeding trucks.

Bicycles are a primary means of transportation. Those without bicycles use the public buses. The buses of the Sri Lanka Transport Board are said to be the cheapest transport in the world. On the other hand, they are crowded and are known to stop and start without the slightest warning. For maneuvering through the streets of Colombo and Galle, the *autochaw*, a three-wheel motor scooter, is popular. The major cities have taxis, of course, but automobiles, in general, are highly coveted because they are expensive as well as hard to get.

SHELTER AND FOOD

The most common type of house is a single-story building made of hardened mud and plaster with a roof of pink tile or palm leaves. The use of mud as a building material makes sense in Sri Lanka since it is resistant to rotting, termites, and fires and is much cooler than stone or brick. Houses are whitewashed and usually contain only a few pieces of furniture. In the villages there are gardens all around the houses, but in the crowded cities there is only room for a garden in the back.

In the main cities, public buildings and the homes of the upper class look like those found in Europe, Canada, or the United States. In attempting to relieve the terrible overcrowding the government has built apartment buildings. It also has encouraged people to leave the cities and settle the sparsely populated areas of the island by offering a free house and land on which to farm.

The staple food of Sri Lanka is rice. For many years it has been necessary to import most of the rice even though it is the island's main crop. The most important beverage is tea. A typical meal consists of rice with a curry. Rice also is eaten with vegetables or dried fish. Fruits such as pineapples, oranges, mangoes, and papaws (papayas) are consumed. This diet lacks iron and protein because fresh fish and meat are rarely or never eaten. Meat is expensive. And fish and meat are both avoided because of religious prohibitions or caste associations.

Dancers perform during one of Sri Lanka's many festivals.

LEISURE ACTIVITIES

Football, called soccer in the United States, is widely enjoyed in Sri Lanka. But the king of sports is cricket, a game the British brought to Sri Lanka. All over the island boys can be found playing cricket along the side of a road or in a forest clearing. Important cricket games are impossible to avoid as everywhere people turn up their radios to hear the broadcast, and loudspeakers in the streets fill public spaces with news of the match. Sri Lanka plays against other countries in both cricket and soccer matches.

Large towns have movie theaters that show American, Indian, and Sri Lankan films. Traditional plays and puppet theater are also popular. But for those who cannot afford either one, Sri Lanka's many and vivid festivals are a time to enjoy. The processions are full of colorful costumes, dances, and music. Festivals are a good time to indulge in an important Sri Lankan passion: setting off loud firecrackers.

Colombo (above) is built at the mouth of the Kelani River. Many consider the harbor (below), built at the end of the nineteenth century, to be one of the best harbors in South Asia.

Chapter 6

INTERESTING CITIES

★ Colombo

COLOMBO

Colombo is the largest city in Sri Lanka. It is the commercial, maritime, and political capital of the country. From a historical or cultural perspective, Colombo is not an especially interesting place compared with the rest of the island. But it is certainly a place of contrasts. All of the ethnic groups are represented. And nowhere else in Sri Lanka do the old and the new mix so completely. High-rise hotels stand near colonial mansions. Supermarkets are as busy as the street bazaars. In public, one sees men wearing Western fashions as well as the traditional sarong. Sports cars, buses, and one-man rickshaws compete for space amid the traffic.

Built at the mouth of the Kelani River, Colombo's prominence derives from the trade that flowed through it to the rest of the world. Arab traders first used it as a port to ship cinnamon grown in the surrounding area. The Sinhalese shipped camphor, sapphires, and even elephants. The Portuguese, arriving at the beginning of the sixteenth century, carved their coat of arms on a rock and established their first port.

The Dutch built a fort that no longer exists. Where it once stood is the downtown area, referred to locally as "Fort." The Dutch kept their slaves, when they were not working, on an island in a lake. The lake was filled with crocodiles to prevent escapes but

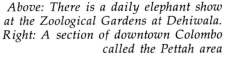

Above: There is a daily elephant show at the Zoological Gardens at Dehiwala. Right: A section of downtown Colombo called the Pettah area

also to provide further protection for the nearby fort. All that remains today is the name of this district: Slave Island. Visible evidence of the Dutch and Portuguese presence is limited today to several churches and an old Dutch cemetery.

Under the British the city became the commercial center of the Indian Ocean. The city grew south along the coast as well as inland. Streets were widened, trees planted, and parks created. Such growth was never foreseen by the first traders to establish themselves at this location. The port at the mouth of the river has long been abandoned. The port of Colombo that exists today is totally man-made. Through it passes 90 percent of Sri Lanka's seaborne trade.

Away from the market district and the extensive neighborhoods where Hindu and Buddhist temples abound, there is Galle Road. Running south along the coast and lined with embassies and

Colombo's town hall (above) and Galle Face Green (right) along the Indian Ocean

modern hotels, Galle Road could be considered Colombo's main street. Between Galle Road and the sea is the large park called Galle Face Green. It is a treeless area that is as often as brown as it is green. The British built it as a seaside promenade, and horse racing was a popular sport practiced there. Today it is the city's favorite place for political rallies, cricket matches, and football games. It is famous as an ideal site to fly kites. The kites, sold right there, soar into the sky on the strong breezes coming off the ocean.

The cinnamon plantations that once existed behind the city are all gone, but a beautiful residential district that occupies the site is called Cinnamon Gardens. It is an area of embassies and government offices. The gardens and huge, overhanging trees that shade the wide avenues have given Colombo the name "Green City."

The port at Galle (top right) was first used by the Portuguese in the 1500s. The walls of the Dutch fort (left) are still standing and the town (right) is within the walls.

GALLE

Galle is the major city of the south. It is a picturesque, quiet, easygoing place. Everywhere there is the presence of history. Its name could come from the Portuguese word for rooster (*galo*), the origin of the first sound the approaching Portuguese heard. Or it could possibly derive from the Sinhalese word for rock (*gala*).

Like Colombo, Galle owes its existence to its port. Its southern location made it a perfect trading location for ships on the Middle East to the Orient route. Its market thrived with goods from all over the world. Its citizens were wealthy and cosmopolitan.

The Portuguese built the first fort in Galle in 1589 after their fort at Colombo had been attacked by Kandyans. In 1640 the Dutch captured the city and tore down, or built on top of, everything Portuguese. The massive Dutch fort, surrounded by

One of the city streets of Galle within the walls of the fort (left) and fishermen working on the beach (above)

the sea on three sides, encloses the town's center. The fort is in almost perfect condition. Most of the older buildings inside are from the Dutch period. Many streets bear Dutch names or names translated from the Dutch. Underneath the fort they built a sewer system that was cleaned each day by the rising and falling tide. They even bred muskrats in the sewers and exported the musk oil these animals produced.

Some ships still anchor in Galle today, including cruising yachts from around the world. However the city lost its position as the main port of the country one hundred years ago when the artificial harbor at Colombo was completed. During World War II Allied seaplanes and Catalina flying boats fighting the Japanese were based here. One of them discovered a large Japanese fleet heading toward the main naval base at Trincomalee on Sri Lanka's east coast. As a result, the Japanese attempt to capture the island failed. This failure is considered a turning point in the war for the control of the Indian Ocean and the surrounding countries.

A busy street (left) and Sinhalese newspapers for sale (right) in Kandy

KANDY

Kandy is unique. It is not a port and there is nothing there that was built by the Portuguese or the Dutch. Situated near the center of the island, it lies in the heart of the hill country at 1,600 feet (488 meters) above sea level. The climate enjoyed by its residents is cool and pleasant.

Kandy comes from the Sinhalese word for hill—*kanda*. It was the capital of the Sinhalese kingdom of Kandy, the only independent part of the island during the rule of the Portuguese and the Dutch. The British finally captured it in 1815. The very late arrival of the Europeans explains why Kandy is the most authentic of Sri Lanka's cities.

In the thirteenth or fourteenth century Kandy became a religious center that grew in importance. Among its monasteries are two old ones that are the headquarters of the two principal Buddhist sects in Sri Lanka. In Kandy is kept the tooth relic, the

Kandy Lake

sacred tooth of the Buddha. Considered Sri Lanka's most prized possession, the tooth relic symbolizes the country's cultural and political independence. It is kept in a large pink temple, the Dalada Maligawa, which has a moat surrounding it. Every August a replica of the tooth is paraded around the city in one of South Asia's biggest celebrations.

The city is surrounded by hills dotted with houses and hotels. Kandy's most famous and, perhaps, most attractive feature is at the very center: peaceful Kandy Lake. It was built quite late, in the nineteenth century, by the last independent king of Kandy. The lake was not popular with the people. In a country where so many reservoirs have been built to irrigate agriculture, it was a real puzzle why anyone would want to develop an artificial lake for the sake of beauty. Additionally, it was built with forced labor, against the wishes of some of the nobles. Together with the British-built promenade around it, it is considered today one of the visual gems of the country.

Above: Trucks bring fruit to be sold at the Kandy market. Left: The gate at the Royal Palace Complex

Kandy has a special status because it is the center of traditional culture. Here Sinhalese music, dance, and arts and crafts are very much alive. There are temples, an archaeological museum, and an Arts and Crafts Center. Most of what was once the Royal Palace Complex, a very large collection of buildings, is gone. But parts of the king's and the queen's palaces still stand and are used as audience halls and the National Museum.

TRINCOMALEE

Trincomalee, on the east coast, is popularly known as Trinco. Its harbor, Koddiyar Bay, has been praised by sailors from many different nations. Horatio Nelson visited it long before he gained fame fighting Napoleon's navies. He proclaimed it "the finest harbor in the world." But what is most striking is its size. It is huge: the fifth-largest natural harbor in the world. Ships are well protected from natural and human enemies. On three sides are

Trincomalee

thirty-three miles (fifty-three kilometers) of hilly shore while on the fourth there are islands.

Trincomalee was a port long before the foreigners arrived. But it was an important religious center as well. The Temple of One Thousand Pillars dates back to before the third century A.D. This temple was revered by Hindus who believed it to be one of the supreme divine residences of the god Siva. Though it was destroyed by the Portuguese, it was rebuilt on the same site, the top of a cliff that drops 360 feet (110 meters) into the ocean. The present temple also is highly regarded.

The city was first occupied by the Portuguese. The Dutch, French, and British fought over it constantly for its strategic value until 1796 when the British finally established permanent control. A considerable number of fortifications and buildings have been left behind by the British. During World War II Trincomalee was

An ox cart delivers kerosene to homes.

the home base for the combined fleets of the Allied powers in east
Asia. Because they were warned of the approach of the massive
Japanese attack in time, most of the fleets were sent out to sea. As
a result there was relatively little destruction. However, the
aircraft carrier *Hermes* plunged burning into the sea about five
miles (eight kilometers) out. Today the wreck is a popular place
for divers to visit.

Trincomalee is a sleepy, local market center. Though important
in times of war, the port is of little economic importance. This
magnificent harbor is located too far from the shipping lanes that
pass to the west and south of Sri Lanka. This may change one day
as the government wishes to encourage shipping companies to use
it.

The composition of Trincomalee's population is rather special. It
is equally divided between Sinhalese Buddhists, Tamil Hindus,
and Muslims. And, like Colombo, it has a relatively large Chinese
minority. An interesting and typical sight is an ox cart delivering
gasoline to gas stations in and around the city.

The Jaffna Peninsula is flat and dry.

JAFFNA

The main port of northern Sri Lanka, Jaffna is better known as the center of the country's Tamil and Hindu culture. It sits on the flat and dry Jaffna Peninsula, which is densely populated and intensively farmed.

Jaffna was the capital of the independent, medieval kingdom of Jaffna that arose as the Sinhalese kingdoms declined. In 1619 the Portuguese arrived. They were followed, as in the rest of the island, by the Dutch (in 1658) and the British (in 1796). The most imposing historical structure still standing is the Dutch fort. It was built, as elsewhere, on top of the Portuguese fort. Situated in the heart of the city, it is a fine example of Dutch military architecture. It is in the classic, five-pointed star shape of eighteenth-century European forts. The sea lies on one side and a moat surrounds it elsewhere. Inside is a Dutch church full of tombstones and monuments, as well as the residence of the Dutch and British commanders.

A canal in the town of Negombo

Jaffna is a market city. The jeweler's district is full of gold, literally, reminding one of a scene from an Arabian Nights movie. The city was especially famous for a certain type of lacelike ornamental work of intertwined gold wires. In the large vegetable and fruit market, Jaffna mangoes are a specialty. They are famous all over the island for their sweetness. And Jaffna's houses are different from others in Sri Lanka because each and every one has a fence around it made of woven coconut or palmyra palm.

NEGOMBO

Negombo, on the coast north of Colombo, is many things. It is a port, a beach resort, a fishing community, and a religious center. Negombo was an important spice port well before the Europeans arrived. The Arabs set up a trading network in which cinnamon was brought to Negombo to be sold and sent abroad. The

Fishermen in a dugout outrigger canoe

Portuguese, besides building the usual fort, left something behind of much greater permanence: Roman Catholicism. Negombo is the center of Catholicism in Sri Lanka. Churches are everywhere. Many of the city's stores sell religious objects.

The Dutch also built a fort, but it too is gone except for the main gate. A few Dutch buildings from the seventeenth century remain as well as a Dutch cemetery. Their lasting contribution, however, was the construction of canals. Beginning in Colombo they stretch 80 miles (129 kilometers) to the north, passing directly behind Negombo.

In Negombo lagoon fishermen abound. They use dugout outrigger canoes similar to those found all over the Indian Ocean and the South Pacific. Nearby, modern hotels and restaurants line the beach. Negombo is a major beach resort of the west coast. The beach is not especially good but its proximity to Sri Lanka's international airport has made it popular with foreign tourists.

An elephant covered in rich fabric carries a replica of the tooth relic.

Chapter 7

THE ARTS

THE PERAHERA AND OTHER FESTIVALS

The people of Sri Lanka love festivals and ceremonies. Some are simple and some elaborate. Almost all are expressions of religious fervor.

The most famous and splendid is the *perahera* "procession" of Kandy. It is perhaps one of the most spectacular in all South Asia. For two weeks in August, an elaborate procession parades around the town each night. At its head is a single monk in yellow robes followed by Kandyan officials in gold-embroidered ceremonial costumes. The central section is made up of elephants covered with ancient, richly decorated cloth coverings, male dancers, whip crackers, drum beaters, flute players, and torch bearers.

Left for the end is a huge, tusked elephant. It carries a replica (for security reasons) of the most sacred object in Sri Lanka—the tooth relic of the Buddha. The relic is in a casket and a covered structure that rests on the back of the huge animal. The perahera's original purpose had been to give the Sinhalese a chance to pay homage to the sacred tooth relic. They still come today from all over the island to do so.

Most Buddhist temples have their own peraheras once a year.

A perahera festival in Kandy (above) and a celebrant walking on hot coals with bare feet (right)

Everyone in the village takes part or contributes in some way. At dusk, these small processions of schoolchildren, drummers, and dancers weave their way through the rice fields.

Another important festival is Wesak. It occurs in May when Buddhists commemorate the birth, enlightenment, and death of the Buddha. At this time, the Sinhalese meditate and listen to monks read the words of the Buddha. But they also hang religious paintings in the streets, each surrounded by colored light bulbs. Lanterns are hung everywhere. In the streets, actors enact Buddhist stories through pantomime in between impromptu concerts of rock music. Colombo's Wesak festival is especially brilliant.

The Kataragama festival is primarily a celebration for the Hindus. It honors the god Skanda in the town of Kataragama. During this celebration Hindus worship at their temples. The streets are decorated with flags and lights. There is a procession as well. Some of the faithful perform painful acts such as piercing their cheeks with miniature spears in order to fulfill vows they have made. Others practice fire walking in which they cross over hot coals with their bare feet.

Men (far left) perform a traditional, vigorous Sinhalese devil dance and women (left) perform a less strenuous dance.

DEVIL DANCING AND KANDYAN DANCE

Like much of Sri Lankan culture, dance is very similar to that of India. But it is sufficiently distinct to have its own characteristics. In India, storytelling and the expression of emotions through dance are communicated primarily by emphasizing hand gestures and facial expressions. Sinhalese dance, on the other hand, uses the movement of the entire body, as well as expert footwork and strenuous acrobatics. Dancing is reserved for men, perhaps because it is so violent. However, to please Western tourists who are not accustomed to seeing men dance by themselves, women are allowed to perform for foreigners.

There are two basic types of dancing. Low-country dancing, often called devil dancing, is practiced along the coast south of Colombo. Up-country dancing, also referred to as Kandyan dance, is practiced in the central highlands. Dancing usually takes place at night when it is cooler. The dancers are illuminated by coconut torches.

Devil dancing is based on ancient rituals that were performed in order to rid sick people of the demons inside them and to ask for help from the gods. Reflecting this past, the demon usually converses with a priest. Besides pure dance movements there is mime, dramatic dialogue, and impersonation. The dancers wear brightly colored masks. The demon, who wears solid black over the rest of his body, uses a mask with bulging eyes, a snakelike tongue, and fangs. The central part of the dance begins when the demon first appears before the audience. One hears the sound of incantations and the beat of drums. In the air is the smell of incense. The demon dancer jumps out, spins around and around and leaps high into the air. Finally he makes a typical movement that consists of twirling the upper part of the body so fast that it is difficult to see.

The other fundamental type, Kandyan dance, is also based on ritual dancing. The dancers wear silver breastplates, anklets, and headdresses. As many as fifty dancers pirouette, skip, and whirl to the beat of drums. At the height of their performance they execute astonishing acrobatics in midair.

CRAFTS

The people of Sri Lanka are skilled at wood carving, mask carving, and metalwork. Wood carving traditionally consists of cutting out chips of wood to form low-relief images. Ancient designs are the basis of the carving that decorates panels, tables, and boxes.

Deeper relief carving and modeling using very light woods are the techniques followed in mask making. The colors originally used were natural dyes produced from plants and minerals.

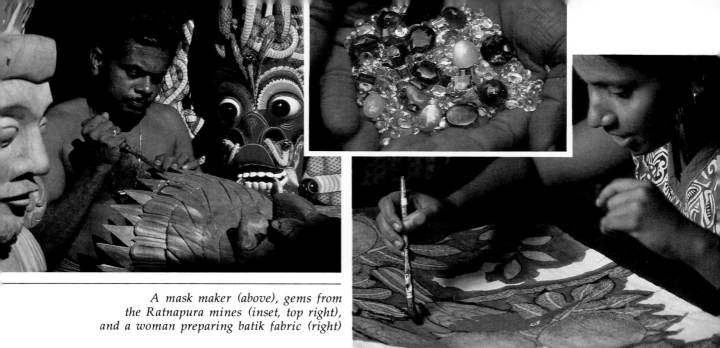

A mask maker (above), gems from
the Ratnapura mines (inset, top right),
and a woman preparing batik fabric (right)

Today, however, brighter enamel paints that are more attractive to
tourists are used.

Sri Lankan metalworkers use a variety of metals: gold, silver,
copper, tin, lead, iron, and various mixtures. One product is
jewelry. Gold jewelry is worn by any woman who can afford to
do so. Brass is important for images of the Buddha, vases, bowls,
and candlesticks.

Other popular forms of craft work include pottery; textiles,
especially batik, a dyed cloth; lace making; and basketry.

GEMS

Since the beginning of time Sri Lanka has been famous for its
gems. Today, it is one of the five most important gem-producing
countries in the world. Good examples may be found far from the
island. A four-hundred-carat blue sapphire from Sri Lanka is part
of the crown of the monarchs of Britain. In New York's Museum
of Natural History there is a beautiful star sapphire called,
incorrectly, "Star of India." It comes from Sri Lanka.

The gems are found in the area of Ratnapura. This means, in Sinhalese, "City of Gems." Over millions of years the gems have been washed down from the central mountains to the lowlands around this town. They are mined in pits dug into the course gravel. Several different types of gems can be found in the same pit, which is quite unusual.

Gemming requires many people, apart from the businesspeople who finance the operation. All workers must be completely trustworthy. Employees are divided into those who do the digging, those who wash off the clay, and those who operate the pump that keeps water out of the pit. The gemmer recognizes which pebbles are true gems. The dealer turns the pebble into a gem by cutting or polishing it. This is usually done on primitive wheels and with bow drills of stick and string.

The most famous gems are the rubies, which are pink or red, and sapphires, which are blue, green, or yellow. The most precious sapphires are the blue ones. Also found on the island are aquamarines, called cat's-eyes. They are considered to be protective charms, which increases their prices. Alexandrites (which change color under different types of light) are common. Yellow topaz, amethyst, garnets, and tourmalines are other Sri Lankan gems. There are no diamonds.

ARCHITECTURE AND SCULPTURE

Buddhism is evident in many areas of Sri Lankan culture. But it achieves perhaps its greatest immediate impact on the outsider through architecture and sculpture. What has been built and carved over the centuries is often large and can be found all over the island. For these reasons, architecture and sculpture are a

Two dagobas in Anuradhapura, with a close-up shot of elephant statues lining the edge

constant reminder of the importance of Buddhism in Sri Lankan society and history.

In terms of size, the most impressive Sinhalese constructions are the *dagobas*. Exceedingly simple in design, they are large mounds of earth that stand as memorials to the Buddha. There can be slight variations in the shape of the mound; for instance, bubble shaped or bell shaped. Over the centuries minor additions have been added. A square box with a furled parasol sticking out of it was placed on top. The parasol is a symbol of royalty in Asia. A square platform surrounds the base, usually with elephant statues lining the edge. Just as Buddhism stresses simplicity and serenity, the dagobas of Sri Lanka are simple, quiet, strong structures.

Dagobas are also very large. They are much larger than similar constructions in India. They overwhelm the viewer with their monumental size. Two in the ancient capital of Anuradhapura are especially large. Their mass and height are equal to the great pyramids of Egypt. The largest of all is considerably higher than St. Paul's Cathedral in London and almost the height of St. Peter's in Vatican City.

Pillars from a Buddhist monastery in Anuradhapura (left) and the ruins of a relic house (above) in Polonnaruwa

Less imposing Buddhist architecture also exists. These are shrines and small buildings where worshipers leave offerings of flowers and incense in front of an image of the Buddha.

The monarchs of the ancient Sinhalese kingdoms of the dry zone built royal palaces. They featured great pillared halls, large open courtyards, and many adjoining buildings for official and private use. These have been in ruins for many years.

Sculpture is frequently linked to architecture. Where this connection is closest is around stairs leading into important palace rooms or buildings. The steps themselves may have relief carving covering them. On either side are slabs of stone called guard stones, each carved in the form of a figure. At the base of the stairs lies a moonstone. This is a semicircular piece of granite carved with bands of decoration surrounding an image of the sacred lotus flower. The bands, in low relief, show symbols associated with Buddhism: elephants, bulls, lions, horses, and geese. Moonstones are found only in Sri Lanka.

The Sleeping Buddha and disciple
Ananda at Gal Vihare Temple in Polonnaruwa

The subject used most often is the Buddha. Relief carvings of the Buddha are common, but more imposing are the statues. The statues followed three basic postures: standing, seated, and reclining. The different gestures of the Buddha's hands have significance for Buddhists. Polonnaruwa is a very important center for Sinhalese sculpture. The statues, which were cut into, or away from, the natural rock, are of very high quality. The most impressive of those that remain is the 46 foot (14-meter) reclining figure of the Buddha. Nearby is the 12-foot (3.6-meter) statue of what some authorities believe to be King Parakramabahu I, who ruled in the twelfth century.

THE FABLED TEA OF CEYLON

Tea from Sri Lanka is famous throughout the world. It has been grown and prepared there for many years. The American author Mark Twain, during his visit in 1896, noted that tea was big business.

Tea growing and preparations are also art. Grown on farms, called estates, on the hillsides of the wet zone, tea production requires skill. Tamil men and boys weed and tend the ground around the bushes and prune the bushes so that they grow no higher than 4 or 5 feet (1.2 or 1.5 meters). At the right moment, Tamil women and girls, with wicker baskets on their backs, walk through the rows of bushes picking the buds and exactly two leaves.

At the factories the tea leaves are first dried. Next, the leaves are crushed to get the sap out. The tips of the leaves are then allowed to ferment on concrete floors and finally roasted in hot driers. These various steps require very careful temperature control, timing, and, in some cases, the humidity in the air must be controlled.

Before the tea is sold, while it is being purchased, and even after the sale, tea tasting is extremely important. Tasting is done by experts who look for differences in quality. Good tasters can not only tell that a mistake was made when the tea was being processed, but sometimes can tell where in the process the tea was damaged.

The tea departs from Sri Lanka in the form of packets or packed in chests lined with tinfoil.

Chapter 8

ECONOMICS AND
POLITICS

A DEVELOPING COUNTRY

Sri Lanka is one of the thirty-six poorest countries of the world. Such poor countries are called developing or Third World countries.

Sri Lanka is poor for a variety of reasons. There are virtually no resources that can be used as fuel or as raw materials for industry: no oil, coal, iron, copper, bauxite (aluminum), or tin. Only graphite and gem stones are found in abundance and some limestone for making cement. The possibility of using falling water to produce electricity exists but it is limited.

Sri Lanka is heavily dependent on agriculture even though large parts of the island, the dry zone, are difficult to cultivate. Sri Lanka sells primarily agricultural products. For many years the declining price of tea on the world market has meant that the country receives considerably less income than before. At the same time, the prices of foreign manufactured goods that are imported have been going up.

Dominating the issue of how to increase Sri Lanka's wealth is the population problem. The mortality rate has been steadily declining. This is due to the mosquito elimination program of the 1940s and better and more widespread medical care in the rural areas. However, too many people means not enough jobs. It also

Opposite page: Waterfalls could be used to produce energy.

means not enough food. Though more rice is grown than any other cultivated plant, each year the government must pay for large quantities to be brought into the country.

What makes Sri Lanka different from other developing countries is the support of the government for the quality of life of its people. The government has spent an astounding amount of the country's resources on health and education. Sri Lanka has an adult literacy rate, life expectancy at birth, and infant mortality rate that are considered equal to countries of middle income. The quality of life is well above that found in other poor countries. This cannot continue. There are not enough revenues to provide this quality of life to an ever-increasing population. And by investing heavily in schools, housing, and sanitation, the government has not been able to invest elsewhere. The roads, railroads, communication, and light and heavy industry that the country needs if it is to climb out of its present economic difficulties are not being built.

In an attempt to remedy this situation, tourism has been greatly developed. Another new source of income comes from Sri Lankans working abroad. From Singapore and the Persian Gulf Arab states, where women from Sri Lanka work as domestics, wages are sent back home to help support their families. And Sri Lanka's unemployment rate goes down slightly as well.

The present political situation in which Tamil guerrillas are fighting for independence has not helped the economy. The clashes between the guerrillas and the army, and the assassinations, have scared off the tourists. Similarly, foreign business executives now think twice before investing. Keeping the armed forces prepared to deal with the guerrillas has added one more cost that the government of this developing country does not need.

Above: Tapping a rubber tree
Left: Picking green coconuts

AGRICULTURE

Agriculture is important in Sri Lanka. Half of the population is employed in farming. Agriculture represents a large part of the country's total wealth and 40 percent of the export revenues.

There are two distinct types of agriculture. One is the plantations originally created by the Dutch and the British. These are large-scale farms, technologically advanced, and occupying a relatively small part of the cultivated land. They grow what Sri Lanka offers to the world's markets. Most important by far is tea, which Sri Lanka produces more of than any other country except India. Though it sells a high-quality, black tea, Sri Lanka has suffered from declining world tea prices. Rubber is the second most-important plantation crop. Coconuts from which come coconut oil, dried coconut meat, and fresh coconut are the third. Minor export plant products are the spices cardamon, cinnamon, citronella oil, cloves, nutmeg, and pepper. The plantations are concentrated in the wet zone.

The other type of agriculture is the production of crops that will feed the people. Farmers grow food to feed themselves and their families. Called subsistence farming, it can be found all over the country. It usually involves very small farms cultivated by peasants using traditional techniques. In Sri Lanka the staple food is rice, so this grain is cultivated to the greatest extent by far. Vegetables such as chilies, onions, potatoes, and maize (corn) also are grown.

For many years Sri Lanka has had difficulty feeding its people. There are years when there is a bumper crop of rice. But just as often there is not enough. Periodic droughts and overpopulation keep the country from reaching self-sufficiency.

This problem is especially acute in the wet zone. Because this is the area where most of the population is concentrated, the population explosion has put tremendous pressure on the available farming land. Relatively large amounts of the cultivated land has always been occupied by plantations that do not grow rice. The population increase has led to larger towns and cities. Thus some of the land previously used for farming now has been covered with roads and buildings.

Because they are passed from father to son, the average size of the farms in the wet zone dropped in the 1950s and 1960s. Many farms became too small to support a family. This problem is made more acute by the social superiority of the farmer caste. Farmers without, or with little, land prefer to feel the pangs of hunger rather than accept other forms of work that they consider degrading.

A bounty of coconuts (left)
and a fresh vegetable market (above)

The government has made an effort to find solutions to these problems. It has established family planning programs and offered high prices for rice and other foods to motivate peasants to grow the maximum. Ambitiously, it has embarked on a plan to restore and enlarge irrigated areas in the unpopulated dry zone.

The first major project in the dry zone was the damming of the Gal Oya River in the southeast. Built during the 1950s and 1960s, the project irrigates 143,320 acres (58,000 hectares). To decrease the population pressure and unemployment in the wet zone, incentives were created to encourage groups of farmers to settle in the project area. Many of the 250,000 wet-zone farmers required training since they had no experience working in the dry zone. In 1969, with considerable financial aid from international organizations, the Mahaweli River project was begun. It is the largest of the dry zone irrigation and land cultivation projects completed so far. A secondary benefit of this project is the hydroelectric power that it has made available. In the mid 1980s, it provided one-third of the country's electricity.

Over half of Sri Lanka is forested but little is used commercially.

A plant that manufactures equipment for rubber mills

INDUSTRY

Manufacturing is not an important part of the country's economy. The processing of agricultural products for export dominates. These tea, rubber, and coconut factories are few in number but quite large. They are owned by the government or foreign businesses. Other factories produce cement, chemicals, paper, textiles, tires, flour, steel, plywood, salt, leather furniture, fertilizer, ceramics, roofing tiles, and herbal drugs. Because of the rising cost of imports, the government has made a special effort to increase the number of consumer goods made in Sri Lanka.

There are also a very large number of small, privately owned businesses. They have few employees and not much capital is invested. These businesses usually produce foods, beverages, and tobacco. Typical products or processes are biscuits, jam, meat preservation, packing and canning, beer, cigarettes, and matches. In order to decrease the high unemployment, the government has actively supported cottage industries. Typical are pottery making, mat weaving, hand-loom weaving, carpentry, jewelry manufacturing, wood carving, and the spinning of coconut fiber. Whether large or small, most factories are located in the cities.

Pottery (left) and textiles (right) for sale

In 1978, the government created an area called a free-trade zone north of Colombo. This was done to encourage foreign companies to construct new industries, which are located in this area. Most of the factories that were constructed produce textiles and garments such as raincoats for export. Garment manufacturing has grown to such an extent that, as of 1986, more money was entering the country from the sale of clothing than from tea. At present, manufacturers that make electrical parts and appliances are the most welcome.

Sri Lanka is the world's leading producer of amorphous graphite, which is found along the southwest coast. Almost all of it is exported in a crude form.

A relatively new industry is tourism. Until 1983, the government successfully attracted tourists by upgrading the quality of transportation, training hotel employees, and giving special advantages to foreign hotel companies that decide to build in Sri Lanka. This has made it easier for tourists to see the island's great beauty, visit the religious and historic monuments, and relax along the incredible beaches.

THE GOVERNMENT SYSTEM

Like quite a few former colonies, Sri Lanka has evolved its own type of government. In 1931, well before independence in 1948, the country became the first Asian state to adopt universal franchise (the right to vote) for women as well as men over twenty-one years of age. The age limit has since been lowered to eighteen.

Sri Lanka's first constitution dictated a form of government that imitated that of Great Britain. The king or queen of Britain was even represented by a governor-general. In 1972, however, a new constitution was written and the country became a republic but remained within the Commonwealth group of countries that once were British colonies and still work closely with Britain.

Sri Lanka has only one legislative body, the National State Assembly. Its members are elected indirectly. The people vote for political parties. The number of votes each party receives determines the number of seats it receives in the Assembly. There is a president who is quite powerful and is elected directly by the people. He or she represents the country at national and international events and appoints the prime minister and the Cabinet. In 1960 Sri Lanka became the first country in modern history to have a woman as head of state: Prime Minister Sirimavo Bandaranaike. For administrative purposes, the country is divided into districts, each with an appointed governor and elected council. The local authorities are the municipal, town, and village councils.

The system of law is rather complex. There exists a Supreme Court, a Court of Appeals, a High Court, district courts, and other local courts. The Common Law is based on Roman-Dutch law.

National State Assembly Building

Commercial law, civil law, and criminal law are based on English law. The Kandyans, Muslims, and Tamils have their own customary laws. The penal code is based on India's code.

Two political parties have dominated the government since independence. One is the UNP or United National party and could be considered conservative or right of center on the political spectrum. Its members, often well educated and English speaking, come from all ethnic and language groups. They believe in Sri Lankan nationalism, parliamentary democracy, and an economy based on private ownership. The other is the SLFP or Sri Lankan Freedom party. It is Socialist or left of center. This group favors Sinhalese nationalism, equality, and government control of the economy. Other, smaller parties also exist.

Almost everyone in Sri Lanka agrees that the government must keep the country's multiethnic and multi-religious character if there is to be peace, cooperation, and economic progress. But at the same time many Sinhalese believe that they should rule Sri Lanka as they did before the Europeans arrived. They are the majority ethnic group. They also see Sri Lanka as the only true Buddhist sanctuary in the world. They believe that their presence in the government will allow them to champion the Buddha's message of peace, tolerance, compassion, and love in a world of conflict and tension.

FOREIGN RELATIONS

Sri Lanka has only one neighbor, but that one is the very large and relatively powerful country of India. An issue between the two countries with historical roots is the citizenship status of the Indian Tamils who work on the tea plantations in the highlands. Essentially, neither country wants these people. In 1964 it was agreed, after many talks, that half would return to India while one-third would receive Sri Lankan citizenship. What to do with the remaining 150,000 Indian Tamils has been discussed for many years. In 1974 India agreed to take half of them and, in 1987, to accept those who remained.

India is interested that Sri Lanka remain a friendly neighbor, since possession of the excellent harbor at Trincomalee by a hostile power would be a blow to India's security. In the 1980s India became actively involved in Sri Lanka's internal affairs. India arranged meetings between the government and violent Sri Lankan Tamils wishing for independence. India at times aided the Tamils and sent troops to the island to help maintain peace. This situation has led to increasing tension between the two countries.

In recent decades Sri Lanka has gained widespread recognition for its neutrality. After World War II the United States and the Soviet Union fought a war of nerves to stop each other from dominating large parts of the globe. Though small and relatively poor, Sri Lanka willingly led efforts by African and Asian countries to stay strictly neutral in this "Cold War."

The country's economic relationships with the rest of the world have complicated matters. Communist China provided the most aid during the early years of independence. In the 1950s, Sri Lanka sent rubber to China—often when it was very difficult to sell rubber to anyone—in exchange for Chinese rice. In the 1970s China sent economic aid. Other Communist countries that helped in constructing factories and with science and technical education were the Soviet Union and East Germany.

Sri Lanka's relationship with the United States has been one of both love and hate. The United States has provided economic support by buying Sri Lanka's rubber and supplying rice. When China became Sri Lanka's preferred trading partner in 1953, the embittered United States cut off all aid. Over the decades this on-and-off association has continued. The United States has aided the country in the areas of health, transport, irrigation, and assistance with food provisions.

In recent years Sri Lanka has become quite close to the Arab world. The Arab countries buy a very large amount of Sri Lankan tea. Also, many Sri Lankans work in Arab countries and send most of their salaries back home. In 1970, as a result, Sri Lanka announced it would end all relationships with Israel, a country that the Arabs have been trying to isolate. The conflict that erupted in the Persian Gulf in 1990-91 had very serious consequences. Thousands of Sri Lankan workers returned home to a country that suffered from excessive unemployment already.

The price of petroleum went up and the demand for tea went down.

Much aid has entered the country lately from such groups as the International Monetary Fund, the World Bank, and the Asian Development Bank. Individual countries that made a special effort in the 1980s were the United States and Japan. Especially important was the Colombo Plan, which allowed thousands of Sri Lankans to receive technical training abroad and permitted visits by numerous experts and trainers from other countries.

THE TAMIL QUESTION

The Sri Lankan mosaic of several cultural and religious groups living together within one state has been increasingly strained since independence. This tension is principally between the majority Sinhalese and the largest minority group, the Sri Lankan Tamils. The Sinhalese wish to dominate the political life of the country and the Tamils do not want to lose what rights and influence they hold. After continuous rebuffs from the Sinhalese, some Tamils lost patience and decided that the island should be split into two independent states; one for the Sinhalese and one for the Tamils, which the Tamils would call *Tamil Eelam*, "Precious Land of the Tamils." Naturally, the Sri Lankan government is not at all interested that this should come about.

Under the British, neither of these peoples had the upper hand. The tension that developed in the 1950s and again in the 1980s can be attributed to a number of factors. The British who, like previous foreign rulers, had enforced peace, were gone. The economic problems that Sri Lanka faced during the last forty years led to greater competition between the groups. This, in turn, led easily to bitterness and finger pointing. There also exists the worldwide force of nationalism. This is the idea that each nation or ethnic group should have its own independent government and state.

During the 1950s, the Tamils became upset with the government's resettlement efforts in the dry zone. The resettled people were Sinhalese for the most part. The Tamils interpreted this action as the expansion of the Sinhalese into an area traditionally belonging to the Tamils, though few Tamils actually lived in the resettled areas. Under the British, a relatively high proportion of Tamils received an education and entered government service. However, after independence, the Sinhalese took over government and professional jobs previously held by, or open to, the Tamils. The Tamils were angered by the blocking of educational and occupational opportunities.

In June of 1956, Sinhalese was made the only official language. Two months later a new group, the Tamil Freedom party demanded an autonomous Tamil area in the north and east within a federal Sri Lanka. They also insisted that Tamil be made an official language. In 1958, after some violence, the Tamil language did achieve this status.

Violence reemerged on a more intense scale and for a longer period in the 1980s. In 1983 a guerrilla group called the Tamil Tigers turned to widespread attacks on the military and Sinhalese civilians. These terrorist attacks led to equally savage attacks by the Sinhalese against Tamils out of revenge. There also have been attacks against the government by radical Sinhalese who believe the government has been far too tolerant of Tamil demands. Attacks on police stations, mutilations, massive riots, disappearances, assassinations, and massacres of villagers became

Government trooops (left) and Tamil soldiers (right)

common. In Colombo, heavily armed troops guarded important government offices. Government officials and journalists received death warnings. Some were shot to death in their homes.

The violence has hurt Sri Lanka. Many Tamil businesses have been destroyed. For this reason, and perhaps also because of Sinhalese jealousy over the predominance of the Tamils in the business world, Tamil businessmen have left the country to settle in India and elsewhere. Many tourists are afraid to spend vacations in Sri Lanka and have stayed away. The government has been forced to spend precious revenues on strengthening the army. Western investment has declined as has the all-important rice production.

India is concerned about the conflict because there are many Tamils in the southern part of that country. In 1983 the Indian

Tamil refugees

government convinced the Sri Lankan government and the Tamil rebels to meet, though the agreement that resulted did not last very long. In 1987 the Indian government and the Indian state of Tamil Nadu provided economic aid to the main Tamil city of Jaffna. This greatly irritated the Sri Lankan government, but later that year the two governments signed the Indo-Lankan Accords. As part of this settlement, forty-seven thousand Indian troops entered the country to enforce a cease-fire and disarm the Tamil rebels. They not only failed to do this but became very unpopular with the people, Tamils and Sinhalese alike. They returned to India in early 1990.

The serenity of Buddhism contrasts sharply with the violence between the Sinhalese and the Tamils.

SRI LANKA'S FUTURE

Between 1983 and 1991 over nineteen thousand people died in this conflict. There is no solution in sight at the moment. The tragedy appears difficult to resolve despite the best intentions of many Sri Lankans. The island has become a place of contradictions. Great natural beauty and an appealing people exist side by side with fear and bloodshed. Buddhism, the religion of serenity, peace, and love, and Sri Lanka's most distinctive feature, is practiced amid violence that is reported in the world's newspapers and television news programs. Sri Lanka's greatness comes from the cultural and religious variety of its many groups of people. These same people must become aware that to allow their rich diversity to continue they must work out the inevitable conflicts that arise. The future of their ancient and lovely country is at stake.

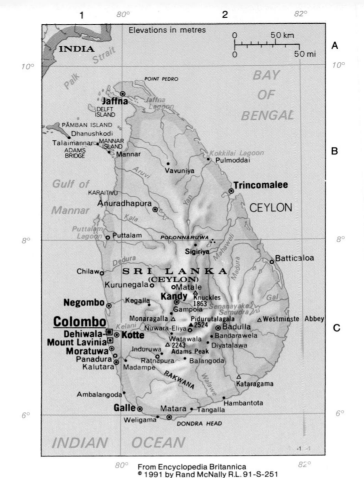

MAP KEY

A cricket match

MINI-FACTS AT A GLANCE

GENERAL INFORMATION

Official Name: Sri Lanka Prajathanthrika Samajavadi Janarajaya ("Democratic Socialist Republic of Sri Lanka")

Capital: Administrative, legislative, and judicial capital is Sri Jayawardenapura, Kotte, a suburb of Colombo since 1982, but the economic and commercial capital is Colombo.

Government: The republic is headed by an elected president, who appoints a prime minister and a cabinet. The president is the chief of state and head of government and is elected for a term of six years. The 225-member Parliament is elected for six years and is responsible for passing the nation's laws. Sri Lanka is divided into nine provinces and 24 administrative districts. Each district is headed by a district minister who is appointed by the president. The highest court is the Supreme Court. Every citizen over age 18 has a right to vote. Sri Lanka is an independent member of the Commonwealth of Nations (British Commonwealth).

Religion: There is no official state religion. The constitution gives freedom of religion for all, but primacy is given to Buddhism. Sri Lanka has been a stronghold of the Theravada branch of Buddhism for centuries. Nearly 69 percent of the people are Buddhist, some 15 percent are Hindu, 8 percent Muslims, and 8 percent Christians. The majority of Sri Lankan Muslims practice Sunni Islam. Most of the Christians are Roman Catholics.

Ethnic Composition: Sri Lanka is a multiethnic, multi-religious, and multilinguistic country. The main ethnic groups are the Sinhalese (74 percent), the Tamils (18 percent), and the Sri Lankan Moors (7 percent). Sinhalese are the descendants of people from northern India, Tamils of people from southern India, and the Moors are descendants of Arabs. Other minor ethnic groups are the Malays, the Burghers, and the Veddahs. Sinhalese occupy most of the southern and central regions while the Tamils are in the majority in the northern and eastern regions. Most Moors speak Tamil and follow Islam. Burghers are the descendants of Europeans settlers who intermarried with Sri Lankans. Veddahs are the original inhabitants of the island.

Language: Official languages are Sinhalese and Tamil. Although the use of English has declined since independence, it is spoken by some 10 percent of the population, largely from the urban educated middle and upper-middle classes.

National Flag: The present national flag was officially hoisted in 1978. There are two vertical stripes of saffron and green, representing the Hindu and Muslim minorities at the hoist side, and to the right there is a maroon rectangle representing the Buddhist majority. The rectangle has yellow bo leaves at the corners and a yellow lion carrying a sword in one upraised paw in the center. The entire flag is bordered in yellow and a yellow narrow vertical area separates the saffron stripe from the maroon rectangle.

National Emblem: The main symbols are the *punkalasa* (a filled vessel), a heraldic lion within a lotus petal border, and the *dhammachakka* (the wheel of the Buddhist doctrine). The sun and the moon and two ears of corn appear on both sides of the filled vessel signifying prosperity, discipline, righteousness, eternity, and self-sufficiency.

National Anthem: *"Sri Lanka Matha"* ("Mother Sri Lanka")

National Calendar: Gregorian: the lunar calendar is used for religious festivals.

Money: The Sri Lanka rupee (SL Rs) of 100 cents is a paper currency. In 1990 one Sri Lankan Rupee equaled $0.0245 in United States currency.

Membership in International Organizations: Asian Development Bank (ADB); Colombo Plan; Commonwealth of Nations; International Monetary Fund (IMF); Nonaligned Movement; South Asian Association for Regional Cooperation (SAARC); United Nations (UN); World Bank; Group of 77; Intersat; Interpol; Inter-Parliamentary Union; World Federation of Trade Unions

Weights and Measures: The metric system (adopted in 1974) is the national standard, but Imperial weights and measures and some local units also are used.

Population: 17,103,000 (1990), 21 percent urban, 79 percent rural. The average population density in 1990 was 675 persons per sq. mi. (261 persons per sq km) — one of the highest in the nonindustrial countries. Most of the population is concentrated along the southwestern edge and in the Jaffna Peninsula.

Cities:
<pre>
Colombo 609,000
Dehiwala-Mount Lavinia 190,000
Jaffna 162,000
Kandy 127,000
Moratuwa 107,000
Sri Jayawardenapura Kotte 102,000
</pre>
(Population based on 1988 estimates.)

GEOGRAPHY

Borders: The pear-shaped island of Sri Lanka is bordered on all sides by the Indian Ocean. Palk Strait separates Sri Lanka from the Indian Peninsula in the north. The total coastline is 748 mi. (1,204 km) long. The country is located only 546 mi. (879 km) north of the equator.

Land: Lowlands constitute about four-fifths of the island, mostly in the northern half and around the coast of the southern half. The coastal plains surround Sri Lanka like a ribbon; in certain sections there are lagoons. The south-central part is hilly and mountainous, ranging in height from 3,000 to 7,000 ft. (914 to 2,134 m) above sea level. One of the best known mountain peaks is Sri Pada or Adam's Peak—sacred to Buddhists, Hindus, and Muslims.

Highest Point: Mt. Pidurutalagala, 8,281 ft. (2,524 m)

Lowest Point: Sea level along the coasts

Rivers: There are some 15 significant rivers, of which the Mahaweli Ganga is the longest (534 mi.; 860 km). Most of the rivers are more than 60 mi. (97 km) long and radiate from the central highlands like the spokes of a wheel. These fast-flowing rivers are important for fish, but not for navigation. There are very few natural lakes.

Forests: About 30 percent of the land is forested and some 20 percent is under natural grasslands. About 3,000 species of ferns and flowering plants grow in Sri Lanka. In the villages and along roads banana, mango, papaya, breadfruit, areca nut, coconut, acacia, palm, satinwood, teak, ebony, and jak trees abound. Coconut and palmyra trees dot the beaches. Orchids, rhododendrons, bougainvillea, and poinsettias blossom all over the island. A reforestation program started in 1970. As a result, export of timber has been banned since 1977.

Wildlife: A wide range of reptiles, birds, and mammals has been greatly reduced as more forestland is converted into rice fields. Water buffalo, deer, bears, elephants, monkeys, crocodiles, and snakes are common. Large and beautiful butterflies abound. Sri Lanka has more than 400 species of birds; many varieties of birds from colder countries spend the winter on the island. Crows, robins, blue kingfishers, mynahs, jungle fowls, hornbills, and green imperial pigeons are common. Wildlife has been protected by law since 1937. Endangered species include the Asian elephant and four species of turtle. Sri Lanka has well-organized bird and game sanctuaries; some one-fourth of the island is reserved for one type of wildlife protection or another.

Climate: The tropical climate has warm temperatures year round. There are no summer or winter seasons as such, but only dry and rainy seasons. The yearly average temperature at sea level is 81° F (27° C) and in the highlands the average is 65° F. (18° C). Almost all rain is caused by monsoon winds. Humidity is high throughout the year. The southwest and central hill country receive 100 or more in. (254 or more cm) of rain annually. The northern, eastern, and southeastern parts receive rains between 50 and 75 in. (127 and 191 cm) annually. Thunderstorms are common.

Greatest Distances: North to south: 274 mi. (441 km)
East to west: 142 mi. (229 km)

Area: Sri Lanka with 25,333 sq. mi. (65,610 sq km) area, is the 24th-largest island in the world.

ECONOMY AND INDUSTRY

Agriculture: Agriculture, employing some one-half of the labor force, is the leading economic activity; it provides about 40 percent of the export revenues. Some one-third of the total land area is available for cultivation. The northern dry zone is flat and requires irrigation to cultivate crops. Tea, rubber, rice, tobacco, spices (cardamom, cinnamon, cloves, nutmeg, pepper), cocoa, and coconut are the chief agricultural products. Tea, rubber, and coconut plantations are located in the central mountainous region. All Sri Lankan tea is black, sorted into various grades. Crabs, prawns, and lobsters are caught along the coasts.

Mining: The island is one of the largest producers of high-grade graphite in the world. It also produces limestone, iron ore, gemstones, and clay. Some 45 varieties of precious and semiprecious gems like blue sapphires, rubies, alexandrites, moonstones, aquamarine, topaz, garnets, amethyst, and zircons have been mined for centuries in Sri Lanka. There are no known deposits of coal, petroleum, copper, bauxite, or tin.

Manufacturing: Paper manufacturing, steel rolling, plywood, sugar refining, chemicals, furniture, fertilizer, roofing tiles, and tire manufacturing are the major industries. Processing of food products, rubber products, cement, leather, textiles, and manufacturing of herbal drugs are also important. To promote industrial development, the government operates a free-trade zone near Colombo and it has attracted many foreign investments. Wood and mask carving, pottery, lace and basket making, hand-loom weaving, carpentry, spinning of coconut fiber, and metalworking are the traditional cottage industries. Processed food products, leather items, and textiles and garments have become very important exports.

Transportation: All parts of the island are easily accessible by trains, buses, or cars. Ownership of private cars is very low—less than 1 percent of the people own cars. Colombo is the center of rail and road transport. It is a major man-made seaport and also has an international airport. Several international airlines serve Sri Lanka. There is a ferry service from Mannar Island (Sri Lanka) to Pamban Island (India) in Palk Strait. Bicycles are a primary means of transportation.

Communication: *Dinamina* and the *Dawasa* are the two principal Sinhala dailies, and the *Daily News* is the principal English-language daily newspaper. The government operates both commercial and noncommercial radio broadcasting services in Sinhala, Tamil, and English.

Trade: The chief imports are machinery and transport equipment, petroleum products, sugar, wheat, and rice. Major exports are ready-made garments, processed agricultural products, tea, rubber, gemstones, and coconuts. The major trading partners are Japan, United States, United Kingdom, Germany, and China.

EVERYDAY LIFE

Education: Public education is free from kindergarten to the university level. Education is compulsory for children between ages 5 and 14. A high percentage of children continue school until the age of 16 or 18. Most of the schools and colleges are owned and run by the government, but a few private schools exist. In the early 1990s there were eight universities and several technical and vocational schools and teacher training colleges. The literacy rate at 87 percent is one of the highest in Asian countries.

Holidays:

New Year's Day, January 1
Tamil Thai Pongal Day, January 14
Independence Commemoration Day, February 4
Sinhala and Tamil New Year, April 13-14
May Day, May 1
National Heroes Day, May 22
Bank Holiday, June 30 and December 31
Christmas Day, December 25

Movable holidays include Maha Sivaratri Day, Good Friday, Diwali, and 'Id al-Fitr. In addition the day of the rise of the full moon of every month of the Buddhist calendar, called a Poya Day, is a public holiday.

Culture: There are a number of university, special, and public libraries. The oldest and the largest library is the Colombo Public Library. The four national museums at Colombo, Kandy, Ratnapura, and Anuradhapura contain collections pertaining to prehistory, archaeology, and ancient art. The Colombo Museum contains the largest known collection of Sinhala palm-leaf manuscripts Sri Lanka's numerous religious processions are full of colorful costumes, dances, and music; setting off loud firecrackers is popular. The *perahera* procession of Kandy, with a replica of the sacred tooth of Buddha, is perhaps the most spectacular procession in all South Asia.

Housing: Houses with mud walls and thatch roofs are common in the rural countryside. Most of the houses are painted white and usually contain only a few pieces of furniture. Many rural families are extended with more than two generations of the same family living together. Elders are respected especially by children. Rural men wear a *sarong* (a wrapped long skirt) and shirt, and women wear a *redde* (long skirt) with a blouse. Some Sri Lankan women also wear a *sari*, a long single piece of cloth wrapped around the body. Many middle and upper class houses are surrounded by a walled compound. Housing shortages are more acute in and around big cities. Colombo has many high-rise hotels, colonial mansions, supermarkets, large parks, and beautiful public buildings.

Food: Rice is the staple in Sri Lankan diet, along with pulses (peas and beans) and nuts. People consume little meat or fish. Buddhists who adhere strictly to religious doctrine do not eat meat of any kind. Hindus do not eat beef and the Moors do not eat pork. Many different curry powders are used in cooking. Fruits such as pineapples, oranges, mangoes, and papayas are consumed. Both men and women chew betel, and both sexes smoke small cigars. Toddy is a popular alcoholic drink. Tea is the most popular drink, taken at almost every meal and also as refreshment.

Sports and Recreation: Many sports introduced by the British such as soccer, rugby, and cricket are very popular. Tennis, squash, badminton, horse racing, kite flying, fishing, sailing, and surfing are popular also. Moviegoing is a favorite national pastime. People enjoy traditional live and puppet theater, especially in the rural areas. The sacred city of Anuradhapura, with numerous Buddhist temples and the sacred bo tree, and the ancient city of Kandy, with its Dalada Maligawa Temple (sacred tooth relic of the Buddha), are the most popular tourist attractions.

Health and Social Welfare: Compared to people of other less-developed countries, Sri Lankans enjoy a relatively high quality of life. Sri Lanka was one of the first developing countries to eradicate malaria and tuberculosis. With a fast-growing population, adequate health and sanitation facilities lag behind. The government-supported health system provides free medical care to all people. In the early 1990s there were some 7,000 people per physician, and 350 persons per hospital bed. The best medical facilities are located near large urban centers such as Colombo. Traditional medicine (ayurveda), supported by the government, enjoys great credibility.

A wide range of social services are provided by the state. These include monthly allowances to disabled, sick, and old persons; relief to persons affected by natural disasters; state-run homes for the aged and the very young; service for the handicapped; maternity costs; and workmen's compensation.

IMPORTANT DATES

500,000 B.C.—Human beings first arrive in Sri Lanka

307 B.C.—Indian prince Mahinda introduces Buddhism to the Sinhalese people

200 B.C.-A.D. 993—Sri Lanka's classical age (the Anuradhapura period)

100 B.C.—Anuradhapura is plundered by armies from south India

55 B.C.—The first group of Sinhala people migrate to Sri Lanka from northern India

A.D. 1505 — Portuguese arrive in Sri Lanka in search of cinnamon and other spices

1589 — Portuguese build the first fort at Galle

1591 — Portuguese conquer the Tamil kingdom of Jaffna

1640 — Dutch capture the city of Galle

1658 — Dutch take possession of Sri Lanka

1796 — British arrive and end the Dutch presence in Sri Lanka

1802 — The crown colony of Ceylon is created

1815 — The British defeat the last independent kingdom of Kandy and unite Kandy with rest of the crown colony of Ceylon

1870 — Tea becomes Sri Lanka's chief export

1896 — Mark Twain visits Sri Lanka

1921 — The Ceylon University college is founded

1931 — British grant Sri Lanka limited self-rule; voting right for every citizen, men and women, over age 21 is granted

1937 — Protection of wildlife starts

1942 — Japanese attack Sri Lanka in an effort to eliminate the British naval bases at Trincomalee and Colombo; University of Ceylon is founded

1947 — United National party wins country's first elections; D. S. Senanayake becomes prime minister

1948 — The Ceylon Independence Act comes into force; Sri Lanka becomes a dominion within the British Commonwealth; Soulbury Constitution of 1946 is adopted as the constitution of Sri Lanka

1949 — The Central Bank is established

1950 — Colombo Plan is launched

1951 — Sri Lanka Freedom party is founded by S.W.R.D. Bandaranaike

1953 — China becomes Sri Lanka's preferred trading partner; the United States cuts off all aid to Sri Lanka

1955—United National party loses general elections; Sri Lanka is admitted to the United Nations

1956—Sinhalese is proclaimed the official language of Sri Lanka; S.W.R.D. Bandaranaike becomes prime minister

1957—Great Britain begins withdrawal from Trincomalee naval base

1958—Tamil-Sinhalese language riots occur

1959—S.W.R.D. Bandaranaike is assassinated by a Buddhist monk

1960—All private schools are nationalized; Sirimavo Bandaranaike, widow of S.W.R.D. Bandaranaike, forms the government and becomes the first woman elected as head of state in the world

1961—Sinhala is made the official language

1963—Barter agreement is reached with the People's Republic of China

1964—Agreement is reached with India over status of Indian Tamils in Sri Lanka

1966—Use of Tamil for official purposes is permitted in Tamil-speaking areas

1969—The Mahaweli River project begins with international aid

1970—United States Peace Corps and Asia Foundation programs are terminated; Sri Lanka announces end to all relationships with Israel

1972—Sri Lanka is proclaimed a republic under a new constitution; all existing universities are amalgamated as the University of Sri Lanka; Tamil United Front is formed

1973—A five-member National Press Council is established

1974—Accord is reached with India over an island in Palk Strait

1975—All domestic banks and plantations are nationalized

1977—J.R. (Junius Richard) Jayewardene becomes prime minister; constitution is amended to establish a strong presidential government; the constitution assures freedom of religion to all, but grants primacy to Buddhism

1978—The present national flag is officially hoisted; the free-trade zone near Colombo is created

1979—A state of emergency is declared in Jaffna as Tamil violence escalates

1981—The government declares a state of emergency for five days as Sinhala-Tamil relations worsen

1982—A new state of emergency is declared; Sri Jayawardenapura Kotte becomes the administrative capital designate

1983—The term of Parliament members is extended for another six years under a national referendum; the state of emergency is ended; South Asia Regional Cooperative (SARC) is established

1985—SARC ratified and renamed South Asian Association for Regional Cooperation (SAARC) by seven South Asian nations including Sri Lanka

1986—Tamil terrorists blow up a plane at Colombo airport

1987—Indo-Lankan Accords signed by Sri Lanka and India. India troops are allowed into Sri Lanka to enforce cease-fire between Sinhalese and Tamils.

1988—Sri Lanka passes legislation extending citizenship to some 230,000 "stateless" Indian Tamils; President Jayewardene announces his retirement from politics

1989—General elections are held; Ranasinghe Premadasa is elected president

1990—Indian peacekeeping force wthdraws from Sri Lanka

1990-91—As the result of the Persian Gulf War, thousands of Sri Lankan workers return to Sri Lanka

1991—Tamil guerrillas are suspected in the murder of Indian prime minister Rajiv Gandhi; between 1983 and 1991 some nineteen thousand people have died in the ethnic violence

IMPORTANT PEOPLE

S.R.D. Bandaranaike (1916-   ), wife of S.W.R.D. Bandaranaike; first elected woman prime minister in the world; twice prime minister (1960-65, 1970-77) of Sri Lanka

S.W.R.D. Bandaranaike (1899-1959), regarded as the founder of Sri Lanka as a Socialist state; prime minister from 1956 to 1959

Dutthagamani (100 B.C.), great ruler of the Anuradhapura period, famous for having saved Sri Lanka from Indian invaders

J.R. (Junius Richard) Jayewardene (1906-   ), elected Sri Lanka's first president in 1978 and reelected in 1982

Kasyapa, king from A.D. 477 to 495, who moved the capital to Sigiriya and built a rock fortress and palace that was considered an architectural and engineering feat

Mahasen (third century A.D.), king famous for building many fine dagobas and other monuments

Mahinda (300-? B.C.), son of King Asoka the Great of India; introduced Buddhism to the people of the island of Sri Lanka

Horatio Nelson (1758-1805), British naval commander who won crucial victories against French

Parakrama Bahu I, the Great (ruled 1153-86), king; built many magnificent structures, unified the government of Sri Lanka, and organized the economy

Ranasinghe Premadasa, (1924-   ), president since 1988

D.S. (Don Stephen) Senanayake, (1884-1952), prominent political figure in modern Sri Lanka, leader of United National party (UNP), and first prime minister of independent Sri Lanka

Dudley Senanayake, son of D.S. Senanayake; elected prime minister in 1965

Siddhartha Gautama (?563-483? B.C.), Indian philosopher, founder of Buddhism, referred to as the Buddha and the Enlightened One

INDEX

Page numbers that appear in boldface type indicate illustrations

About the Author

Robert Zimmermann was born in Lima, Peru, and has lived in Thailand, Britain, Spain, and Portugal as well as the United States. He received a B.A. (Cum Laude) from Clark University and an M.A. from George Washington University, both in geography. For the past sixteen years he has lived in Chicago where he teaches world geography and twentieth-century world history in a private high school. In 1982-83, Mr. Zimmermann spent a year in Nassau as a Lecturer in Geography and Social Studies at the College of the Bahamas. He has published a map of Chicago for tourists and a journal article on a course he teaches about Russia and Austria. Recently he was given the Award for Excellence in Teaching Geography by the Geographical Society of Chicago.